Cook and Feast

GENERAL NOTES

The cup measurements in this book are US cups.

My choice of products for daily cooking and my catering business reflects my food philosophy: food should be as natural as possible with no artificial colouring or preservatives. I look for products that are unadulterated and natural in flavours. These include naturally brewed Kikkoman soy sauce and Megachef Premium Oyster Sauce. Make your own stocks. If you have to use stock cubes and powders, avoid those with preservatives, monosodium glutamate and too much salt. Instead, choose those with only natural products.

Cover photograph by Ben O'Donnell (www.benjaminodonnell.net)

Text copyright © 2018 Audra Morrice
Food photography copyright © 2018 Ee Kay Gie

Published by
Landmark Books Pte Ltd
5001 Beach Road,
02-73/74
Singapore 199588

Landmark Books is an imprint of
Landmark Books Pte Ltd

ISBN 978-981-4189-90-3

Printed in Singapore

COOK AND FEAST

Audra Morrice

◇LANDMΔRK◇BOOKS◇

To my family, Carl, Alex and Andre.

Thank you for your patience, your understanding
and for being my pillars in life.

CONTENTS

Preface

I already knew what the title of this, my second book, was to be when I was autographing my first cookbook. So, for those of you who have my first book with "Cook and Feast" written in it, you know I'm telling the truth! As for the contents, it was always going to be about cooking and feasting, the two things in life that brings great joy to me and to many.

Over the past six years, I've dedicated my life to food. It has become my career and by this I mean not just catering for an event or creating recipes to fill up the pages of a book. My aim has always been to put a smile on people's faces by presenting delicious food to them. As cooks and chefs, we pressure ourselves in wanting to please others. But what I have received in return was something far greater.

Feasting for me is not only about vibrant colours and flavours that make you go "ooooooo yum", but also expressions of celebration, pleasure, delight, joy and plentifulness. At the same time, it is a gathering of people, the crossing of boundaries, the path to creating new connections, to understanding better what we don't know.

In this book, I've celebrated my heritage and made connections with other cultures. This has resulted in recipes that reflect all of them. I've brought to life memories of my travels, of people I've met, of conversations I've had, places I've visited, of birthday celebrations, of food my family absolutely adores, of my obsession with banana leaves, *gochujang* (Korean hot pepper paste), stoneware vessels and so on. I've disregarded conventions and trends, and brought to life the purity and simplicity of vegetables and grains and their possibilities to be the centerpiece at a feast.

For all those that I have cooked for, you've welcomed me with open arms into your homes and into your kitchens. You've introduced me to your entire family and your friends. You've trusted me and opened your minds and palates to food of my heritage and my style of cooking. Most importantly, you've shared your culture, your beliefs and a big part of your life with me. Thank you for making me a part of your celebrations and your memories.

I am lucky to be surrounded by a whole lot of incredibly wonderful and talented people,

and specially want to thank:

Ben O'Donnell, a Sydney-based producer and filmmaker (www.benjaminodonnell.net) took the photos on the cover and next to the Preface of this book. Thank you for your unwavering support and valuable perspectives. Your belief in and support for me and my philosophies are so greatly appreciated.

Vera Lye, a friend of 30-something years and a remarkable journalist and beautiful writer, for being the sister I never had, providing me with open, honest and precious views.

Lisa Zahra, an exceptional interior designer (www.lisazahradesign.com.au) with a unique talent for detail and a friend of 15 years, lent me her beautiful linen and crockery for photography and, more importantly, shared her most valuable perspectives of design.

Zoe Pollitt, founder and creative director at Eskimo Design (instagram @snowyzoeeskimo), so dynamic and creative, not to mention so very generous with her knowledge, expertise and time, has been a friend and support in so many ways and helped immensely with some of the party photography.

Jo Lam, a friend of 15 years and the passionate founder of Orli (www.orli.com.au), allowed me to ransack her kitchen drawers for beautiful tableware.

Vivien Macintosh, founder of Vivi Designs (www.vividesigns.com.au) and a friend of 18 years, for having the biggest heart, one with such a vibrant spirit, was so generous with her time and perspectives.

Kim Udler, a great friend and Director at Laing and Simmons, Randwick, a beautiful soul, so generous with her time.

Jenny Granger, Leona Fell, Juanita Baldwin and Danielle Cesana for being such great sports.

The good folk at TeraNova Tiles on Bronte Road, Waverley, for generously lending ceramic and stone tiles as backgrounds for photography.

And finally, to all my friends and family who have tirelessly supported me, thank you for sticking by me. I love you all.

Cook and Feast is a celebration of delicious food, of simple produce, of culture, of vibrant colours and the gathering of people. Through this book, I hope you will create your own experiences and an abundance of special memories.

Audra Morrice
September 2018

Cook and Feast

My parents, John and Stella, used to entertain quite a lot. Throughout my early childhood, I witnessed countless feasts prepared single-handedly by my mother. Freshly grated coconut squeezed by hand to make coconut milk, curries cooked in massive Indian urns, hours and hours spent deboning chicken wings to make them look like little lollipops, then marinated, dusted with flour and deep fried, buckets of vegetables cut into sticks of the same size ready to be blanched bit by bit in piping-hot, pickling liquid then squeezed in muslin straight after to make the *achar* we so loved, kilos and kilos of vermicelli fried to perfectly al dente – and so on. She would easily cook for 100 guests at a time.

People never witnessed the days of preparation leading up to the dinner. The aromas coming from the kitchen whetted their appetite, and feasting on dish after dish of abundant, delectable food brought out to the table gave them pure joy.

Dinners like these would start with a plan. What Mom decided to cook was often driven by what people liked to eat. She knew her guests well and pleasing them was an easy task. From there, she would visit her regular butcher, seafood stall and so on at the markets. Mom knew all the vendors as friends, so she often received the best price for the best produce one could find. She was exceptional at using all ingredients, wasting none.

My mother was the epitome of both skilled chef and charming host. Between the kitchen and the garden where the dining tables were laid out, she would manage the service wearing two hats: the executive chef, so to speak, running the pass and directing the flow of food, and the gregarious hostess who dazzled everyone with her wit and infectious giggle – doing all this often beautifully clad in a dress she designed and sewed herself. Mom cooked a range of cuisines. Though a full-blooded Chinese, she cooked some of the best Indian curries, so say many of her Indian friends and acquaintances. My Dad was always proud of her.

For many people, cooking for friends and family isn't quite the romantic affair one reads about in the spreads of magazines, or watches on TV today. The idea of cooking for large numbers of people is scary and generally sends them into a bit of a panic. For some, preparing daily or even weekend meals are a stress point. Yet, when you have happy and well-fed people at the table, it is incredibly satisfying, certainly worth the effort in the kitchen.

The things I learnt from my mother, from cooking for my family, and from running my own catering business boils down to just one word – organisation – a word which is key from start to finish.

Start by selecting a menu that works together not just in terms of tastes but also in the cooking processes. Then focus on being organised in the preparation of ingredients and dishes, and the rest will flow.

Week-night meals at home

We all live busy lives. I totally understand that, in this day and age, everyone wants everything quickly, including our dinners. Traditionally, dinners were not just a time to eat to be nourished, it was also a time of gathering when family members would catch up, unwind, and chat while sharing a meal they prepared together at home. Sadly, most of us have lost this cultural practice. Home-cooked meals have become less important and hence less time is allocated to them. As a result, we turn to eating out, leading to not just poorer diets but, more significantly, also becoming disconnected with where our food comes from.

For many, especially those who work long hours, week-night meals have become a chore and lobbed into the basket labelled "too hard". So, we say: "I don't feel like cooking. I don't know what to cook. What are we going to have for dinner tonight?" Trust me, I've been there – many times.

It doesn't have to be like that. The best advice I can give about week-night meals is to keep them simple. Simplicity will take the stress out of cooking and you will start to enjoy the process.

A combination of protein, vegetable and a carbohydrate, or a high-protein vegetarian combo is more than sufficient. Perhaps focus on one-dish meals then gradually build from there. In any case, keep it straight forward on weekdays and leave the special dishes to the weekends. For busy moms and dads who are keen to cook healthy meals for the family, if it all still seems too daunting, start with cooking on the weekends or just one night a week.

Here comes the word again – organisation. It is crucial to plan and prepare ahead of time. Spread the jobs across several days and you'll find it doesn't become a mammoth task. Don't be afraid to delegate. Give the children easy tasks. I remember always being given the job of picking the tails off bean sprouts. I'm sure just about every Singaporean kid went through this back then. It was, honestly, the most laborious job ever for a child, but I also remember mom and I sitting at the kitchen table working our way through a mountain of bean sprouts and having the best conversations. Mom would often also get me to dust meats in flour, which she then proceeded to fry. At other times, she gave me the simple task of peeling vegetables. All these small and easy activities made me feel I was needed and contributing to family life.

My ability today to effortlessly fold dumplings and char siu buns wasn't something I acquired overnight. It came with years of working alongside my mother, watching, learning and practicing. Marinating meats, rolling meatballs in between palms, rinsing and chopping vegetables, peeling fruit, kneading dough, cleaning up – all these jobs are easy and can be done by young ones. I can't speak any louder about the value of getting children used to helping in the kitchen early in life. It fosters an important and essential life skill – cookery.

The best thing about cooking at home is it allows you to feed your family well while managing the budget. Before the start of the work week, think about what you'd like to eat for that one or two home-cooked meals during the week.

Allocate time to shop for the ingredients you need in the weekend, ensuring that your pantry is always stocked with staples. Purchase fresh meat which can take you through the first couple of days of the week.

What I sometimes do is to buy meat in bulk, portion them according to different dishes, wrap them well and freeze. So when I decide on what I'd like to cook, I simply pull the relevant package out in the morning or leave it to thaw overnight in the fridge. Another strategy is to slow braise meat dishes during the weekends enough for several meals. Portion and pack them away in the fridge or freezer and simply heat them up when required.

Doubling up on the presentation and use of certain dishes is something I do all the time. A simple braised beef or pork dish I serve up tonight along with some rice and stir fried vegetables can be shredded up and tossed with noodles for an entirely different dish tomorrow.

If you're anything like me, I will only purchase seafood super fresh. So, if you haven't got much time to shop for seafood during the week, pick them up on weekends, and clean, prep and store them in the coldest part of the fridge ready for cooking the following day.

The gist of it all is to get organised and allocate time to prepare hearty, wholesome meals for the week. Trust me, a little thought will go a long way. Get creative! There are lots of great recipes in this cookbook that can be whipped up quickly or prepared ahead and frozen for times when you have no time to cook but just have enough energy to heat a dish up.

As I have said, you just need to be a little organized.

Having family and friends over

Just like cooking everyday meals for the family, the process of preparing a dinner party for four or a dozen people kicks off with a well-planned menu.

At least a week before the party, work out what you are going to cook. It's really important to know your guests, their likes and dislikes, what they can and can't eat. So, before you decide on a menu, find out if anyone has food restrictions and what they love to eat. Not all dishes have to exclude items on the restricted list; just make sure there are enough dishes that everyone can enjoy. Do take care in separating food allergens during preparation and cooking. Most South East Asian dishes don't contain dairy, and diet-compliant products such as gluten-free soy sauce are easy to find these days.

The basic rule of thumb is to ensure that the dishes you decide on compliment in flavours. The easiest way to achieve this is cooking by cuisine. Selecting all Chinese dishes, Indian dishes or Italian dishes will ensure a good blend of flavours. However, as you start to understand families of flavours associated with specific cuisines and those that sit in between, you will then also be able to achieve a seamless flow of flavours across different food cultures.

I find it easiest to keep a common thread of ingredients to link dishes.

For example, soy sauce, oyster sauce, Shaoxing wine, sesame oil and Szechuan peppercorns are prevalent in Chinese cooking. Malay cuisine, on the other hand, are more heavily weighted towards using fresh aromats and sauces like kecap manis (Indonesian sweet soy sauce), and Peranakan cuisine sits nicely in between the two with the inclusion of soy, fermented soy beans, cinnamon, cloves, lemongrass, belacan (shrimp paste), candlenuts, galangal and turmeric.

In deciding what to cook for dinner parties, another extremely important factor is to ensure your cooking processes flows smoothly so that all your mains can be served at the same time. Choosing four dishes that need to be cooked a la minute on the stove is a challenging task and is not the wisest decision. So choose carefully. Select a combination of cooking methods so that you can cook multiple dishes at the same time and all dishes are piping hot when served. Try steaming or poaching, with braising or roasting, and top it up with a stir-fry dish that will come together quickly on the stove.

Your decision on what dishes to cook also depends on how you intend to serve the meal. Whether it's buffet style, shared plates or individually plated, ensure you have the right vessels and serving utensils needed.

Here are some menus that allow you to prepare much in advance, and use different methods of cooking to produce dishes with flavours that complement each other. The last thing you want is to be slaving over the stove instead of spending time welcoming and socialising with your guests. Don't forget, you're the host, hence the life of the party!

Menu 1
Beef and Lettuce Rolls with Chilli Honey Miso (pre-prepared, quickly seared, page 27)
Salmon, Kimchi and Herb Dumplings (pre-prepared, poached, page 91)
Bean Sprouts, Chilli and Herb Salad (pre-blanched, page 113)
Monk Fish Stir-Fried with Fermented Black Beans (stir-fried quickly, page 101)
Sticky Black Bean Chilli Pork Ribs (oven-roasted, page 48)
Braised Szechuan Beef Brisket (braised, page 33)

Menu 2
Beef Carpaccio with Pickled Onions (pre-prepared, page 24)
Grilled Barramundi with Sambal Matah (oven-grilled, page 80)
Audra's Tauhu Goreng - Crispy Tofu with Peanut Sauce (shallow-fried, page 132)
Sticky Gula Melaka Tempeh with Kaffir Lime (stir-fried quickly, page 136)
Slow-Baked Satay Pork (oven-baked, page 57)

Menu 3
Spiced Buttered Couscous (pre-prepared, page 119)

Spiced Smoked Eggplant with Grated Coconut (fired quickly, page 106)
Fried Cabbage with Mustard Seeds and Chilli (stir-fried quickly, page 105)
Fish with Coconut Green Masala in Banana Leaf (steamed/chargrilled, page 86)

So what about dessert? Well, many can be made a day or two in advance, and truly, if you end a fabulous meal with some store-bought favourite sweets such as cakes, pastries, fruit and ice cream, I'm sure your guests will be just as delighted!

So how do you pull off these menus? Here's a plan to execute Menu 2 for the days leading up to the dinner.

You can start preparing two days before or at the least one day prior. Remember also to delegate where you can, this will take a little more stress away from you and the evening will flow much more smoothly. Whether it's your partner, a good friend or family members, allocate jobs that can be done easily by others.

Menu
Beef Carpaccio with Pickled Onions
Grilled Barramundi with Sambal Matah
Audra's Tauhu Goreng – Crispy Tofu with Peanut Sauce
Sticky Gula Melaka Tempeh with Kaffir Lime
Slow-Baked Satay Pork

1-2 days before
Run through your recipes and jot down the list of ingredients you need and go shopping.
Marinate the satay pork overnight, refrigerate.
Cook the peanut sauce for the tofu, refrigerate.

1 day before
Pickle the onions for the beef carpaccio, refrigerate.
Prepare ingredients for the tempeh, refrigerate.
Prepare and bake the satay pork, cool and refrigerate.

On the morning of the dinner
Purchase the barramundi.
Prepare the banana leaves for the fish dish.
Marinate the fish and wrap in the banana leaves, keep in the fridge.
Make the *sambal matah* for the fish dish.
Season and prepare the carpaccio and plate it. Cover with clingfilm and refrigerate.
Prepare all other toppings – pick the herbs, crush the peanuts, slice the chillies and radish etc.
Shred the cucumber for the tofu dish, refrigerate.
Chill water and wines if you haven't already done so.

Early afternoon

Set the table and floral arrangement if any.

Prepare your ice buckets for drinks.

Prepare all serving dishes and utensils. These should be considered before cooking so you can efficiently plate up dishes as soon as they are cooked and also to make sure that the layout on the table works.

Late afternoon

Cook the rice and keep it warm.

Have a shower, be beautiful, and have a well-deserved drink.

An hour before your guests arrive

Get someone to fill the ice buckets with ice.

Remove the plated beef and other condiments from the fridge and let it come to room temperature.

Cover the satay pork with foil and reheat in the oven on medium temperature.

Reheat the satay sauce and keep it warm.

Fry the tofu, and keep it warm.

Stir fry the tempeh, keep it warm.

Just before dinner

Crank up the heat and bake the fish.

Remove the foil from the pork and allow to char a little in the same oven as the fish.

Finish the carpaccio dish with topping.

Add the final touches to all other dishes.

Serve and bask in the compliments!

Works of Art

There are some dishes that clearly have the wow factor. They impress guests because of their sheer extravagance, how colourful they are, or that they require diners to assemble or cook them at the table. Sometimes, generous portions will also do the trick. Whatever it is, always choose a platter or bowl that will enhance the dish and present it in all its glory.

Here are just a handful of dishes from this cookbook you can use to create an impressive feast. Just let your creative juices flow when plating them!

A beautiful and large platter of Beef and Lettuce Rolls with Chilli Honey Miso (page 27).

A luxurious platter of Spiced Buttered Couscous (page 119) topped with Indian Slow-Roasted Spiced Lamb (page 67), scattered with ruby pomegranate seeds, toasted almonds and fresh coriander.

A massive platter of several Baked Trout with Herb and Black Rice Stuffing (page 76). The Birthday Trifle (page 160) doesn't need any help to show indulgence and extravagance. The Sugee Cake with Cinnamon Sugar (page 176) from a beautiful bundt tin will leave your guests speechless.

Some of the best dining experiences we've had with friends were when we invited them over for Teppanyaki or Steamboat (pages 68 and 70). Absolutely everything is done before your guests arrive but there is no prior cooking required! All the raw ingredients are plated, wrapped in cling film, and stacked up in the fridge. The table is set with all utensils needed, the grill plate or steamboat pot is made ready. When your guests are assembled, all the food is brought out and arrayed on the table and everyone is involved in the cooking. I couldn't think of a better way to celebrate food with friends.

Adding a little bit of store-bought magic to the table

I have mentioned store-bought food to complement your home-cooked offerings. There is no rule to say you can't buy your favourite cakes, ice-creams, exotic fruits and so on from specialty shops to complement what you have prepared yourself. The key word is 'complement', so choose wisely. This approach will take a bit of pressure off the kitchen.

As a starter, freshly shucked oysters or cold seafood platters are good choices. Add a dash of home-cooking by complementing the oysters with your own dressing. Several of the dressings in this cookbook will go well (pages 24 and 96) and it will lend a special touch that people will remember. As a host, bring that platter of oysters around the room so you get to meet and chat with all your guests. Remember, people are there to be with you. The more they see you, the greater the success your dinner will be.

If guests bring food items as gifts, plate them up and serve them if they work with your menu. They will certainly be pleased by this.

Table Settings

Depending on the look and feel you are aiming for, think about how you'd like to set the table. Jump on the Internet or flip through magazines and pinch ideas of styles that you like. Over the years, I have moved from matching absolutely everything to using an eclectic mix of stoneware to achieve a contemporary, organic look.

If you're planning to have a shared-plates dinner, it's probably best to keep the setting simple so as not to clutter the table. Still, you should have appropriate dinner plates, bowls, utensils, water glasses and wine glasses, if using.

I prefer not to overcrowd the table with a range of wine glasses. Prepare them and leave them in the kitchen or nearby on a sideboard. Should your guests decide to move from white to red wines, simply replace their white wine glasses with the red's.

Placemats provide contrast to the table top. Invest in good linen napkins with subtle colours. For a touch of flair, make your own napkin rings. For example, tie napkins with some butcher's twine and aromats like cinnamon quills, or use fresh herbs like rosemary and thyme.

For buffets, ensure that the table is the perfect size and decorated to give an impression of abundance (this must not to be confused with clutter). Tasteful additions of fresh greens, flowers and citrus always freshen up a table.

Serving platters and utensils should work with your dinner plates. They don't need to be of the same make but should complement well. Remember that you don't want to create a cluttered, clumsy environment to detract from the glorious food you are serving.

Floral Arrangements

Feel free to place a beautiful floral arrangement in the middle of the table but make sure that it is one that can be easily removed and placed elsewhere when you are ready to serve.

If you have a large and wide rectangular or square table and there is too much empty space after the food is laid out, use floral arrangements, potted herbs and flowering plants or even candles and table decorations appropriate to the theme of the food served to fill the space - but again, be mindful not to create clutter.

Unique Edible Gifts

Like children at parties, adults also like receiving gifts. I love receiving edible gifts so a really lovely gesture is for everyone to go home from your dinner party with a little gift of food. Guests will appreciate it especially if they know it's homemade by the host.

Choose edible gifts that can be made weeks in advance. So, once again, get organized early. Consider cookies, meringues or miniature bundt cakes or brownies. Infused oils are easy to make. Purchase beautiful but functional bottles, add rosemary or dried chillies and garlic or all three and allow to infuse. Homemade sambals, pickles or preserves also make good gifts.

I have a stack of quaint glass jars at home, sterilized and stored well. When certain fruits are in season, say strawberries, they go straight into the pot and the jars are filled when the mixture is piping hot. Lids go on, and I have a stock of strawberry jam ready to give away at my next dinner party.

Whether you choose to give cookies, cakes or jams, dress them with beautiful boxes or ribbons and attach a personalised thank you note of friendship.

A friend once gave me a vintage bottle with a hand-written recipe of her favourite vinaigrette scrolled up and tied to the neck. What a splendid idea! I keep the recipe on my fridge door and I have a beautiful bottle of her vinaigrette in my fridge. I smile every time I look at the recipe or taste the dressing. What a lovely, lasting and unique gift!

Cook and Feast

Food has the immense power of bringing people together. To cook and feast, however simple or extravagant, whether with friends, family or acquaintances, is a privilege and one that all should indulge in frequently. It's a way to unwind and relax, a way to develop relationships, a way to stay connected – it's a way of showing our love. It is one of life's greatest pleasures and an experience that brings such great joy to all.

Beef Carpaccio with Pickled Onions

SERVES 4

This dish is inspired by something I tasted during a trip to San Francisco some years ago. It is based on getting your hands on the best quality meat. It's fresh, herbaceous and a feast for the eyes!

Most of the preparations for this dish can be done a few hours ahead, including the slicing and thumping of the beef. Add the dressing and the toppings just when you are about to serve.

250 g (8.8 oz) good quality beef eye fillet (tenderloin), sinew and excess fat trimmed, rolled
1 teaspoon black peppercorn, toasted and coarsely ground
1 teaspoon Szechuan peppercorns, toasted and coarsely ground
1 teaspoon sea salt
Olive oil

DRESSING
3 tablespoons freshly squeezed lime juice
1 tablespoon fish sauce
1 tablespoon sweet chilli sauce
1½ teaspoons finely minced garlic
1½ teaspoons finely chopped hot red chilli
3 teaspoons finely chopped coriander stems

TOPPINGS
1 small red onion, peeled, halved, sliced thinly with a mandolin and pickled quickly
1 red chilli, finely sliced into rings
2 small red radishes, thinly sliced with a mandolin
2 tablespoons of each micro herb (coriander, celery, purple shiso, radish)
1 tablespoon roasted peanuts, coarsely chopped
1 tablespoon crispy shallots
1 tablespoon crispy garlic

Place the piece of eye fillet on cling film. Wrap and roll firmly until you get a nice even log shape. Hold onto the excess cling film at each end and roll the meat several times in a forward motion until you get a firmly packed little log. Refrigerate for 2-3 hours or overnight.

Scatter the black pepper, Szechuan pepper and salt over a chopping board or a clean bench top. Remove the cling film and roll the beef back and forth over the seasoning, pressing it in gently, then rub all over with 2 tablespoons of olive oil.

Place all the ingredients for the dressing in a clean glass jar, cover tightly, and shake vigorously until well combined.

In a glass bowl, mix 2 tablespoons each of water, white vinegar, sugar and a pinch of salt. Stir until the sugar and salt dissolves. Toss in the onion slices and leave to pickle for at least 30 minutes.

Heat a large, heavy-based frying pan or flat-surfaced cast iron pan on very high heat. Sear the beef on all sides for 1 to 2 minutes. I like a little more variation of doneness so tend to sear the edges a little more. Remove and set aside to rest for 5 minutes. Slice the beef very thinly but ensure that the pieces remain whole. To get it paper thin, place each slice between two clean plastic sheets such as Glad's Go-Between and thump gently with a rolling pin. Gently place each slice flat on a large serving plate. Drizzle over the dressing then scatter over the chillies, pickled onions, radish, micro herbs, peanuts, crispy shallots and garlic. Serve immediately.

Indonesian Braised Beef

SERVES 4

Here, beef is slowly braised till beautifully tender in a rich sauce of kecap manis, tamarind and aromats.
Perfect over hot, steamed rice.

800 g (1.8 lbs) chuck steak,
  excess fats trimmed, cut into
  4 x 6 cm (1.5 x 2.5 in) pieces
5 tablespoons kecap manis
  (Indonesian sweet soy sauce)
2 ripe tomatoes, cut into
  8 wedges each
1 tablespoon (25 g) tamarind
  pulp, soaked in 125 ml (½ cup)
  water, rendered and strained to
  obtain tamarind liquid
5 whole cloves
1 small (4 cm, 1.5 in) cinnamon
  stick
Oil
Sea salt to taste

SPICE PASTE
6 cloves garlic, crushed,
  skin discarded
1 medium (150 g, 5.3 oz) onion
10 g (0.4 oz) ginger
10 g (0.4 oz) galangal
5 candlenuts
2 stalks lemongrass
2 teaspoons ground coriander
⅛ teaspoon ground cumin
1 teaspoon freshly ground black
  pepper
½ teaspoon ground nutmeg
½ teaspoon ground mace

Prepare the spice paste by blending all the ingredients for the paste together.

In a large, heavy-based saucepan or Dutch oven, add 3 tablespoons of oil and place over medium high heat. Fry the spice paste, stirring frequently, until fragrant.

Add the pieces of beef and toss to coat. Add the kecap manis, tomatoes, tamarind liquid, cloves and cinnamon along with another 125 ml (½ cup) water. Mix well and bring it back to the boil, then cover with the lid. Reduce the heat to simmer for about 2 hours or until the meat is very tender.

You will need to check. If too much liquid has evaporated, add a little more water, about 60 ml (¼ cup) at a time. Adjust seasoning with more salt if required.

You can also cook this in a 170°C (338°F) oven for the same amount of time.

Beef and Lettuce Rolls with Chilli Honey Miso

MAKES 15 ROLLS

A wonderful way to eat this is to arrange all the ingredients on a beautiful, large platter and have guests help themselves and build their own bundles of deliciousness. This is a real social dish with lots of vibrant, fresh vegetables!

250 g (8.8 oz) beef eye fillet
   (tenderloin), thinly sliced

MARINADE
1 tablespoon soy sauce
½ teaspoon freshly cracked
   black pepper
½ teaspoon gochugaru
   (Korean red pepper)
½ teaspoon sesame oil
Pinch of raw sugar

CHILLI HONEY MISO
30 g miso
30 g gochujang
   (Korean Hot Pepper Paste)
1 tablespoon honey
1 tablespoon mirin

LETTUCE ROLLS
50 g (1.8 oz) dried vermicelli
   (bean thread noodles), soaked
   in hot water until softened
2 eggs, made into thin omelette,
   rolled, sliced into thin strips
1 bunch shiso (perilla leaves)
8-12 whole oak lettuce leaves
1 large carrot, peeled, julienned
2 stalks spring onions, finely
   sliced on the diagonal
1 cup fresh bean sprouts, tailed
1 medium cucumber, peeled,
   seeds removed, julienned
1 bunch watercress, younger
   shoots and leaves only
4 small red radishes, finely sliced
6 cloves garlic, peeled, thinly sliced
1 large red chilli, finely sliced on
   the diagonal
4-6 large nori sheets, quartered
½ cup kimchi

Start by marinating the beef by mixing together the beef, soy sauce, pepper, gochugaru, sesame oil and sugar.

Then make the Chilli Honey Miso by mixing all its ingredients together until smooth.

Arrange all the ingredients for the lettuce rolls on a beautiful, large platter. When you're about ready to serve, sear the beef briefly in a super-hot pan until just coloured. Remove immediately, place on a side dish and add to the platter.

Provide guests with their own plates and chopsticks to serve themselves from the platter. The idea is to take a lettuce leaf and top it with a nori sheet and slice of beef. Smear on the Chilli Honey Miso, then pile on some of each of all the other ingredients. Roll up and enjoy!

Note: You can substitute the perilla leaves with mint leaves.

Grilled Skirt Steak with Coriander Chimichurri

SERVES 4

Invest in good-quality meats for this dish. Skirt steak is a flavoursome cut but often thought of as being tough. Just ensure it's nicely seared over high heat to char the outside, not overcooked and given time to rest before serving. Most of all, make sure you slice the beef thinly across the grain. This will shorten the length of grain and give you a lovely tender finish.

500 g (1.1 lbs) skirt steak,
    all membrane and sinew
    trimmed, leaving a little fat
Sea salt
Freshly cracked black pepper
Olive oil

CHIMICHURRI
2 chilli padi or Thai scuds,
    finely chopped
½ teaspoon dried chilli flakes
1 large red chilli, finely diced
1 heaped teaspoon chopped
    fresh oregano or ½ teaspoon
    dried oregano
½ cup chopped fresh coriander
½ cup chopped fresh parsley
1 lemon zest
2 tablespoons lemon juice
2 tablespoons champagne or
    white wine vinegar
Good pinch of sea salt
Pinch of raw sugar
4 tablespoons oil

Season the steak well with salt and pepper. Generously drizzle over a good amount of olive oil. Set aside at room temperature.

To make the chimichurri, mix all the ingredients together and allow to infuse.

It doesn't take long to cook skirt steaks, but you need intense high heat. So, use a good cast iron grill that will withstand very high heat or preheat your clean barbecue to a super-high temperature.

As soon as the cast iron grill starts to smoke, cook the steaks on both sides to medium rare. You want a good char on both sides. This should only take about 3 minutes on each side but the exact timing obviously depends on the thickness of your steak. To be sure, grab a cooking thermometer and measure the internal temperature; it should be between 50-55°C (122-131°F) for medium rare. Anything more than this will give you a tough result. Cover loosely with foil and rest the steak for about 8-10 minutes before serving.

To serve, slice thinly across the grain and drizzle with chimichurri. Serve with some kalette sautéed in garlic and chilli.

Slow-Cooked Braised Beef with Green Peppercorns

SERVES 4

Green peppercorns, with their fresh, peppery flavour, is a great ingredient. The ones used in this recipe are brined, but feel free to use fresh ones.

800 g (1.8 lbs) flat cut beef brisket with 0.5 cm (0.2 in) of fat on top
6 cloves garlic, crushed, skin discarded
10 g (0.4 oz) ginger, peeled, sliced
2 large hot red chillies, halved lengthways
2 stalks lemongrass, bruised
8 kaffir lime leaves
1 tablespoon brined green peppercorns
1 teaspoon black peppercorns
3½ tablespoons kecap manis (Indonesian sweet soy sauce)

Preheat your oven to 120°C (250°F) degrees.

Pat dry the beef with paper towels. Add 2 tablespoons of oil in a medium-sized, oven-proof casserole dish or Dutch oven and place over medium-high heat. Sear the beef until brown on all surfaces. Remove and set aside.

In the same dish, add the garlic, ginger, chillies, lemongrass, kaffir lime leaves, green and black peppercorns, kecap manis and 250 ml (1 cup) of water. Bring to the boil.

Return the beef fat side up to the braise and place in the middle of the dish, ladle over some of the braising liquid and cover snugly with foil or cover with a lid. Cook in the oven for 5 hours until super tender. Remove the foil, turn the meat over, then increase the temperature to 220°C (425°F) degrees and roast for a further 20-30 minutes.

Remove the beef from the dish, loosely cover with foil and set aside to rest. Place the casserole dish over high heat on the stove and reduce the sauce until slightly thickened.

Slice the beef thinly (about 1cm, 0.4 in) or shred apart, pour over the chunky sauce and serve with rice and stir-fried vegetables.

Braised Szechuan Beef Brisket

SERVES 4

A beautiful, slow-braised brisket infused with fragrant aromats, this dish can be shredded and served with noodles or rice. The flavours of the braise will develop more when kept overnight.

1.5 kg (3.3 lbs) beef brisket, fats trimmed, leaving a layer of fats
6 cloves garlic, crushed, skin discarded
25 g (0.9 oz) ginger, halved and crushed
1 large onion (200 g, 7 oz)
Spanish red onion, peeled, cut into wedges
1 cinnamon stick
2 star anise
4 cloves
2 tablespoons Shoaxing wine
60 g (2 oz) rock sugar, crushed
2 tablespoons black vinegar
2 tablespoons dark soy sauce
2 tablespoons light soy sauce
2 tablespoons fermented chilli broad bean paste
2 ripe tomatoes, quartered
2 spring onions, cut into 8-cm lengths
Oil

Preheat your oven to 180°C (355°F) degrees.

In a casserole dish, just a little larger than the brisket, heat 2 tablespoons of oil over high heat. Sear all sides of the brisket until lightly golden.

Add the garlic, ginger, onions, along with the cinnamon, star anise and cloves. Deglaze with the Shaoxing wine. Then add the rock sugar, black vinegar, dark and light soy, bean paste, tomatoes, spring onions along with 500 ml (2 cups) of water. Ensure all or most of the beef is submerged in liquid.

Bring it to the boil. Cover and cook in the oven for 15 minutes, then lower the heat to 160°C (320°F) and cook for a further 3 hours or until the brisket is very tender, turning over halfway through.

Note: I like using a cast iron pot (e.g. Le Creuset) to cook this dish as it retains the heat well. Alternatively, cover your casserole snugly with foil.

Pulut Lemper

Sticky rice with sambal chicken filling wrapped in banana leaves

MAKES 8-12 PARCELS

Whenever I return to Singapore, I head out looking for Pulut Lemper. These spiced chicken with sticky rice logs wrapped in banana leaf are incredibly delicious and I absolutely love them. The banana leaf is key as it imparts a special fragrance to the rice.

POACHED CHICKEN

450 g (1 lb) chicken breast
2 cloves garlic, crushed, skin discarded
2 slices ginger
1 large stalk spring onion, cut into 6-cm (2.4-in) lengths
Pinch of salt

SAMBAL

5 large dried red chillies, soaked in hot water until softened, drained, roughly chopped
4 fresh large hot red chillies
4 cloves garlic, peeled
2 candlenuts
1 medium (150 g, 5.3 oz) Spanish red onion or 8 small red shallots, peeled
2 stalks lemongrass, white root-ends only, roughly chopped
½-1 teaspoon sea salt
½-1 teaspoon sugar
4 large kaffir lime leaves, finely chopped
Oil

POACHED CHICKEN

Bring a small saucepan of water with the garlic, ginger, spring onion and salt to the boil. Submerge the chicken breast into the water and bring it back to the boil. Turn off the heat, cover and leave the chicken to cool in the stock. Alternatively, season the chicken breasts lightly with salt, place in a vacuum bag along with garlic, spring onions, ginger and 1 tablespoon olive oil, seal and cook sous vide at 62°C (145°F) degrees for 1 hour. Then remove and shred finely.

SAMBAL

To make the sambal, blend all the ingredients, except the salt, sugar and kaffir lime leaves, to a fine paste. In a medium-sized saucepan, add 4 tablespoons of oil and cook the paste until fragrant and dry. Season with ½ teaspoon each of salt and sugar. Remove 1 heaped tablespoon of cooked sambal and set aside. Toss into the saucepan the shredded chicken and kaffir lime leaves. Adjust seasoning with another ½ teaspoon each of salt and sugar or to taste. Set aside.

FILLING

To cook the fragrant spiced filling, place the coconut, gula Melaka, salt and water in a small saucepan and cook over medium heat until the coconut has softened slightly and all the water has evaporated. Remove from the pan and set aside. In the same saucepan, add a tablespoon of oil. Fry the chillies and the chopped dried prawns until fragrant. Include the reserved tablespoon of sambal and stir to combine, then toss in the coconut followed by the kaffir lime leaves. Adjust seasoning with salt if necessary. Remove from heat, then stir through the crispy shallot.

STICKY RICE

For the sticky rice, prepare your steamer by bringing the water to the boil. Drain the soaked glutinous rice well. Empty into a baking dish, sprinkle over ¼ teaspoon

SPICED FILLING
50 g (1.8 oz) shredded dried
  unsweetened coconut
  or 70 g, 2.5 oz freshly grated
  coconut
25 g (0.9 oz) gula Melaka
Pinch of salt
150 ml (0.6 cup) water
2 large green hot chillies, finely
  sliced into rings
10 g (0.4 oz) dried prawns,
  soaked in water for a few
  hours, then chopped coarsely
  in a blender
1 tablespoon of above sambal
4 kaffir lime leaves, finely
  chopped
1 heaped tablespoon crispy
  shallot
Oil

STICKY RICE
300 g (10.5 oz) glutinous rice,
  soaked in water overnight
¼ teaspoon ground turmeric
Good pinch of salt
2 pandan leaves, knotted
5 tablespoons coconut cream

Banana leaves for 8-12 parcels
8-12 kaffir lime leaves
Extra 8-12 tablespoons coconut
  cream
String
Toothpicks

ground turmeric, tuck the pandan leaves in the rice and steam for 10 minutes. The rice should now be a little glossy. Fork through to separate the grains and steam for a further 8 minutes, then turn off the steamer. While the rice is still hot, pour over the coconut cream and add the salt. Stir through and leave covered to infuse.

WRAPPING
Cut the banana leaves into 8 pieces of 20 x 20 cm (8 x 8 in) or smaller if preferred. Run each piece briefly over an open flame to soften the leaves. I do this over the gas stove. Divide the rice, chicken and coconut mixtures into 8 equal portions (or more if you are making smaller parcels).

Spoon on a portion of rice on each banana leaf, then put some filling and chicken on either side of the rice. Spoon a tablespoon of coconut cream over the chicken mixture, place a kaffir lime leaf on the rice, then wrap the parcel securely and tie both ends with strings or use toothpicks to secure. Repeat with the remaining ingredients.

COOKING
Bring the steamer back to the boil and steam the parcels for about 5 minutes on high, then remove them and grill over an open flame until the leaves are slightly charred. This will impart some smokey flavour into the parcel. I find it easiest to sit a rack over a gas stove and rest each parcel on the rack directly above the flame. Alternatively you can barbecue them.

Serve hot or at room temperature. You can prepare the parcels in advance. After wrapping them, refrigerate them and pull them out to steam and grill as and when required.

Opor Ayam

Coconut and chicken yellow curry

SERVES 4

Opor Ayam has it's origins in Central Java, Indonesia. It uses similar aromats as a Nonya curry but is a very light dish; the sauce is almost broth-like and lovely over steamed rice.

1 whole chicken (about 1.5 kg, 3.3 lbs), cleaned, cut into 12 pieces
4 tablespoons oil
800 ml (3⅕ cups) coconut milk
5 kaffir lime leaves
2 teaspoons sea salt
1 teaspoon raw sugar

SPICE PASTE
15 g (0.5 oz) galangal, peeled, roughly chopped
10 g (0.4 oz) fresh turmeric, peeled, roughly chopped
10 g (0.4 oz) ginger, peeled, roughly chopped
1 large onion (200 g, 7 oz) or equivalent in red shallots, peeled, roughly chopped
4 cloves garlic, peeled, skin discarded
3 large red chilies, roughly chopped
4 candlenuts
2 stalks lemongrass, white root-ends only, roughly chopped
1 heaped tablespoon ground coriander
1 teaspoon ground cumin
1 teaspoon white pepper

Prepare the spice paste by pounding all its ingredients together in a mortar and pestle or blending in a food processor until a smooth paste forms.

Heat the oil in a large saucepan over medium–high heat. Add the spice paste and fry for a few minutes until fragrant. Add the chicken pieces and toss to coat.

Add the coconut milk and kaffir lime leaves. Season with salt and sugar, and adjust according to taste.

Bring to the boil, then lower the heat to simmer and cook uncovered for about 30 minutes or until the chicken is cooked through.

Serve with hot, steamed rice.

Orange-Glazed Roast Chicken with Brown Rice and Quinoa Stuffing

SERVES 4

There is always room for one more roast chook recipe! This one is brilliant with a lovely, nutty stuffing and lots of fresh oranges. If kumquats are in season, do toss some into the dish.

1 free-range, whole chicken (1½ kg, 3.3 lbs), soaked in brine overnight

GLAZE
7 tablespoons orange juice
Zest of 1 orange
3 tablespoons grape or date molasses
1 tablespoon pomegranate molasses
2 Thai red chillies, slit down the middle
1 star anise
2 cm (0.8 in) cinnamon stick

FOR BAKING
1 small (100 g, 3.5 oz) Spanish red onion, peeled, sliced thinly
3 cloves garlic, crushed
¼ orange, sliced thinly
2 cm (0.8 in) cinnamon stick
1 tablespoon olive oil

RICE STUFFING
½ cup cooked al dente brown rice
2 tablespoons cooked al dente quinoa
2 tablespoons pine nuts, toasted
1 tablespoon dried currants
1-2 dried figs, sliced thinly
Zest of half an orange
¼ orange, in segments
¼ teaspoon ground cumin
Good pinch of sea salt
1 heaped tablespoon chopped fresh coriander

To brine the chicken, fill a glass bowl large enough to fit the bird with water and add 1 tablespoon of salt. Stir to dissolve. Submerge the chicken in the water, cover with cling film and refrigerate overnight.

Remove the chicken from the brine, drain well and pat dry with paper towels. Lightly salt and rub 1 tablespoon of oil all over the chicken. Set aside.

Preheat your oven to 180°C (355°F) degrees.

Place the ingredients for the glaze into a small saucepan and bring to the boil. Cook until thick and syrupy. Set aside to cool.

To bake, prepare a baking dish slightly larger than the chicken. Toss together the onion, garlic, orange slices and cinnamon stick with olive oil and place at the bottom of the baking dish.

For the stuffing, toss together all ingredients. Gently spoon the stuffing into the cavity of the chicken, making sure not to stuff it too full or to compress it too much. Lift the bird by both legs up and give it a shake to settle the stuffing. Close the cavity with the flaps of skin at the mouth of the cavity.

Place the chicken on top of the aromats and bake in the oven for 1 hour 35 minutes. In the last 20 minutes of cooking, baste the chicken with the glaze every 5 minutes, pouring the remaining glaze over the chicken in the last 5 minutes. You'll find that the first baste does not really stick but it will improve from the second basting. Remove from the oven and rest before serving.

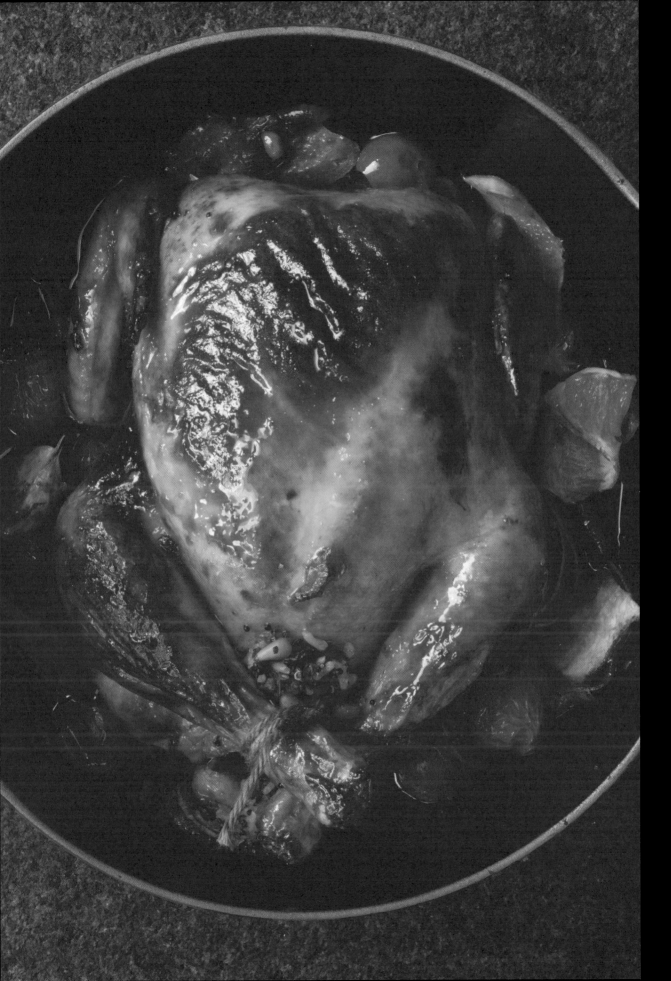

Duck Ragu

SERVES 4 -6

This is a dish inspired by an unforgettable meal at Rafael restaurant in Lima during my trip to Peru in May 2018. The homemade pasta torchio, with luscious duck ragu made with Pinot Grigio, resulted in an insanely delicious dish. The first mouthful was decadent, the second and third just brought tears to my eyes. I know this sounds over the top but it was that good. I couldn't wait to rush home to create a similar dish.

The hero of the dish is, of course, the duck. I suggest that you serve it with some pappardelle pasta, either store-bought or home-made, sprinkled over with pangrattato. However, this duck ragu is just as good sitting over a bed of simply cooked puy lentils.

PANGRATTATO
2 slices of sourdough bread, torn into small pieces
Olive oil
2-3 crushed garlic, to taste
1 sprig fresh thyme
1 small bunch fresh parsley, finely chopped
Zest of ½ lemon (optional)

RAGU
5 duck legs (about 1.2 kg, 2.6 lbs), cleaned and patted dry
2 tablespoons olive oil
1 large (200 g, 7 oz) onion, peeled, finely chopped
2 small or 1 medium leek, finely diced (about 2 cups loosely packed)
6 cloves garlic, crushed, skin discarded
1 cinnamon stick
3 star anise
3 sprigs rosemary
2 bay leaves
2 large dried red chillies
2 tablespoons tomato paste
4 tablespoons sherry or aged port
250 ml (1 cup) Pinot Grigio, any dry, white wine
800 g (1.8 lbs) tinned tomatoes
250 ml (1 cup) veal or chicken stock
Freshly cracked black pepper
4 rashes smoked bacon, finely chopped
Sea salt

PANGRATTATO
Preheat your oven to 180°C (355°F). Toss together the bread, oil, garlic and thyme in a mixing bowl, lay them out on a baking tray lined with greaseproof paper and bake for 10 minutes or until lightly golden. Remove and cool.

Remove 1 or 2 of the roasted garlic according to taste and pour the toasted bread mixture into a food processor and blitz 2-3 times until very coarsely ground. Tip it back into the mixing bowl, toss through the parsley and set aside until ready to use. You can also add the zest of half a lemon to the pangrattato along with the parsley.

RAGU
Reduce the oven to 150°C (300°F). Heat a large oven-proof casserole dish or Dutch oven with 2 tablespoons of olive oil over medium heat. Add the duck legs and brown all over for about 10 minutes. This will also help render the excess fat. Remove the legs and set aside.

Into the same dish with the rendered duck fat (remove some if preferred), add the chopped bacon, fry for a couple of minutes then put in the onions, leek and garlic and cook for about 5 minutes until softened. Toss in the cinnamon, star anise, rosemary, bay leaves and dried chillies. Increase the heat a little, stir in the tomato paste, then deglaze with the sherry followed by the white wine. Stir in the tomatoes, stock and lots of fresh black pepper and a pinch of salt.

Return the duck legs to the pan. Cover, bring to a simmer, then braise in the oven for 2 hours, turning the legs over halfway through. Alternatively, you can simmer the dish covered for 2 hours, stirring every now and then and turning the duck over halfway.

STORE–BOUGHT PASTA
500 g (1.1 lbs) pappardelle

HOME–MADE EGG PASTA
500 g (1.1 lbs) "00" flour
5 eggs

Pecorino, shaved or grated
Extra virgin olive oil
Parsley

Remove the duck legs from the dish, taking care as the meat will literally fall off the bones. Shred the meat into chunky pieces, discarding the fat and bones. Return to the dish and simmer uncovered for a further 10 minutes.

PASTA
If you are using store-bought pasta, cook it in boiling, salted water until al dente during the last 10 minutes of cooking the ragu. Drain, keeping some of the cooking liquid of the pasta aside.

If you are using home-made pasta, start making it while your duck is cooking in the oven. First, sift the flour into a large basin or onto a clean bench top. Make a well in the middle and crack the eggs into it. Using a fork, starting from the middle, slowly incorporate the flour into the eggs until it comes together to form a big mass. If using a basin, transfer it onto a clean bench and start kneading, making quarter anticlockwise turns with each push and stretch. Work the dough for about 8-10 minutes or until the dough is smooth. Wrap in cling film and set aside to rest.

Set up your pasta machine on a clean, spacious edge of your bench top. Divide the dough into two balls. Flatten with your palm, set the pasta machine to the widest setting and start feeding the dough through. Laminate the dough by folding into three, then feed the open end through the pasta machine. Repeat this lamination process a few more times until the pasta is smooth and silky. You are now ready to roll out the pasta into sheets. Reduce the dial down to the next one and feed the pasta through again and again until you get to the smallest setting or your preferred thickness.

Dust the rolled out pasta sheets generously with flour, cut them into long parppadelle strips using a pizza cutter or a curly edge cutter.

Ensure your ragu is bubbling away before you cook the pasta. Cook the pasta in boiling, salted water for only about 2 minutes. Fresh pasta does not take long to cook.

Using tongs, transfer the pasta into the pan of ragu. Toss well to coat, adding a little of the cooking liquid if the sauce is a little dry. Serve topped with pecorino shavings, olive oil, pangrattato and parsley. *Magiamo!*

Korean Grilled Pork

SERVES 4

My interest in Korean ingredients almost became obsessive after a visit to Seoul and Busan with Mom a few years ago. The markets were vibrant, people were friendly and the varieties of kimchi just blew us away. Tofu hot pot with lots of spicy kimchi was a dish I had daily. The other favourite was a good Korean barbecue. It's fun and such a great way to eat. Meats, marinated in a combination of gochujang (fermented hot pepper paste), garlic, sesame oil and soy were grilled on a hot plate then eaten with fresh lettuce, raw garlic, rice and more hot pepper sauce. What more can I say!

600 g (1.3 lbs) pork neck, sliced
   thinly across the grain
2 tablespoons oil

MARINADE
3 cloves garlic, peeled, coarsely
   grated
15 g (0.5 oz) young ginger,
   peeled, coarsely grated
2 large spring onions, finely
   sliced
2 tablespoons mirin
3 tablespoons gochujang
   (Korean hot pepper paste)
2 teaspoons sesame oil
1 tablespoon soy sauce
1 tablespoon sake or
   dry white wine
1 tablespoon gochugaru
   (Korean crushed red pepper)
1 tablespoon raw sugar

SUGGESTED ACCOMPANIMENTS
2-3 cups cooked short grain rice
8-12 oak or other lettuce leaves
2 large nori sheets, cut into 8
   portions each
1 cup kimchi

In a medium glass bowl, mix all marinade ingredients together until well combined. Toss in the pork and mix to combine. Leave to marinate for 2-3 hours or refrigerate overnight.

Prepare a hot grill or a barbecue and bring to high heat. Add 2 tablespoons of oil to the meat, toss well, then grill the meat for a couple of minutes on each side until just cooked and nicely charred. Ensure all the marinade is cooked with the meat.

A great way to serve this dish is to take a piece of lettuce, top with nori sheet, rice, kimchi then a piece of meat and gobble! I particularly love the cucumber kimchi which is crunchy and fresh!

Note: This marinade works really well with chicken as well. I like using chicken thigh fillets.

Sticky Black Bean Chilli Pork Ribs

SERVES 4

Pork is one of the meats I really love to cook with. The ribs are an exceptionally delicious cut and really easy to cater for large groups of people. It's marinated, roasted in slabs and finally sliced into individual ribs. Imagine serving them up on a large wooden board, sticky, salty, sweet, spicy and very moreish!

1 kg (2.2 lbs) slab pork ribs, cut into 4 pieces

MARINADE
20 g (0.7 oz) ginger, peeled and coarsely grated
4 cloves garlic, peeled and coarsely grated
2 tablespoons Shaoxing wine
2 tablespoons soy sauce
4 teaspoons black vinegar
2 teaspoons kecap manis (Indonesian sweet soy sauce)
2 heaped tablespoons black bean chilli sauce
1 teaspoon white pepper
2 teaspoons brown or raw sugar
½ teaspoon liquid smoke (optional)

SAUCE
2 tablespoons Shoaxing wine
2 tablespoons soy sauce
4 teaspoons black vinegar
2 teaspoons kecap manis (Indonesian sweet soy sauce)
2 heaped tablespoons black bean chilli sauce
1 tablespoon brown sugar

Pinch of coarsely ground Szechuan pepper
1 sprig spring onions, finely chopped
Lime cheeks (optional)

Mix all the marinade ingredients together and marinate the ribs with the mixture in a non-reactive bowl for a few hours or overnight in the fridge. Remove from the fridge 30 minutes before cooking.

Preheat your oven to 180°C (355°F). Place the ribs along with the marinade in a roasting tray lined with foil. Cover snugly with foil and bake in the oven for 1½ hours. Remove the foil and increase the temperature to 210°C (410°F). Bake for a further 30 minutes. This will help reduce any excess liquid and give the meat a really lovely char.

While the ribs are baking, mix all the ingredients for the sauce. Heat up a wok till it is piping hot. Once the ribs are ready, slice them up. Pour the sauce in the hot wok, add the ribs and toss until well coated. You'll have to work really fast so make sure everything is ready for this stage of cooking.

Finally, tip in the Szechuan pepper, toss to mix and plate up. Finish off with a sprinkling of spring onions. Serve with lime wedges, if using.

Note: Fu Chi and Lao Gan Ma are good brands of black bean chilli sauce.

Black Pepper Pork Curry

SERVES 4-6

Black Pepper Pork Curry is quintessentially Sri Lankan, though the Chettinads in South India will claim they have some of the best pepper curries in the region. The spiciness in this dish comes from what else but the black pepper! It's very peppery but incredibly moreish and mouth wateringly delicious!

1.6 kg (3.5 lbs) pork neck or boneless and skinless pork shoulder, diced into 4-cm (1.5-in) cubes

SPICE MIX

8 green cardamom pods, crushed, seeds reserved, husks discarded
3 teaspoons black peppercorns, toasted
8 Kashmiri dried chillies, toasted
5 cloves, toasted
1 teaspoon coriander seeds, toasted
2 teaspoons cumin seeds, toasted
1 teaspoon ground turmeric

Cold-press, extra-virgin coconut oil
10 cloves garlic, peeled, thinly sliced, julienned
40 g (1.4 oz) fresh ginger, peeled, thinly sliced, julienned
5-7 large green chillies, sliced on the diagonal (seeds optional)
2 stalks curry leaves
2 large brown onions, peeled, halved, thinly sliced
1 cinnamon stick, toasted
6 ripe tomatoes, halved, cut into wedges
1 tablespoon malt vinegar or black vinegar
1 teaspoon brown sugar
1 teaspoon sea salt or to taste
Coriander, chopped

Prepare the spice mix by grinding together the cardamom seeds, black peppercorns, Kashmiri chillies, cloves, coriander seeds and cumin seeds into a powder. Empty into a bowl and add the ground turmeric. Add water a little by little to form a wet paste.

In a Dutch oven or heavy-based saucepan, add 2 tablespoons of coconut oil and heat over high heat. Sear the pork until brown all over. Remove and set aside. In the same pan, add another 2 tablespoons of coconut oil and cook the garlic, ginger, chillies, curry leaves and onions until golden and lightly charred.

Add the wet spice mix along with the cinnamon stick and cook for a few minutes. If the mixture is a little dry, add another tablespoon of coconut oil.

Return the pork to the pan, followed by the tomatoes and vinegar, brown sugar and salt. Stir to combine. The mixture will seem relatively dry but don't be tempted to add any water. Don't worry, it will come right!

Cover and lower the heat to simmer for 1 hour. Remove the lid, give it a good stir to release any bits that have caught at the base then simmer uncovered for a further 30 minutes or until the pork is tender and the sauce has thickened. Adjust seasoning to your taste if required.

Scatter some freshly chopped fresh coriander on the curry and serve it as part of a shared meal.

Chargrilled Chilli Pork

SERVES 4

Delicious Chinese-style marinated pork tenderloin thrown on the grill! You'll absolutely love it! It's very easy but be patient and allow time for the marinade to infuse into the pork.

600 g (1.3 lbs) pork tenderloin, sliced into 3-mm (0.1-in) thickness

MARINADE
1 tablespoon oyster sauce
1 tablespoon soy sauce
1 tablespoon Shaoxing wine
½ teaspoon freshly cracked white pepper
1 heaped tablespoon Lao Gan Ma chilli sauce
1 teaspoon raw sugar
4 cloves garlic, peeled, coarsely grated
15 g (0.5 oz) young ginger, peeled, coarsely grated
1 heaped tablespoon chopped coriander stems
1 heaped tablespoon chopped spring onions
2-3 tablespoons oil

Mix all marinade ingredients in a glass or ceramic bowl then toss the pork through to marinate for a few hours or overnight in the fridge.

Heat a grill or barbecue till hot. Grill each slice of pork for a couple of minutes on each side until nicely charred and just cooked. Remove and serve immediately as part of a shared meal. Alternatively, fry very quickly in a piping hot wok.

Note: This recipes works well with pork neck or chicken thigh fillets too. I use made-in-China Lao Gan Ma brand chilli sauce for this dish. It's full of crispy onions, chillies and Szechuan peppers. For alternatives, look for chilli sauces that are cooked with dried crispy chilllies.

Masala-Spiced Roasted Pork Shoulder

SERVES 6

Pork neck and shoulder are two cuts of meat which I love using. Flattening out the shoulder by scoring will give you more surface area for the meat to char and caramelise.

1.5 kg (3.3 lbs) boneless pork shoulder
2 sprigs curry leaves
1 large onion, peeled, halved, thinly sliced

SPICE PASTE
1 cup chopped coriander stems, roots and leaves
4 cloves garlic, peeled, coarsely grated
1 heaped tablespoon coarsely grated ginger
1 teaspoon ground black pepper
1 teaspoon ground cumin
½ teaspoon turmeric powder
1 teaspoon hot paprika or chilli powder
½ teaspoon ground cinnamon
2 teaspoons ground coriander
⅛ teaspoon ground cloves
4 green cardamons
1 heaped tablespoon tomato paste
2 tablespoons cold-pressed, extra-virgin coconut oil or vegetable oil
1 teaspoon sea salt
1 teaspoon raw sugar

Prepare the paste by blending all the ingredients together until smooth.

Skin the pork, and trim the fats, leaving some on. Pierce the pork with a sharp knife. Place in a ceramic baking dish, pour over the marinade and massage well. Cover tightly with cling film and marinate in the fridge overnight.

Preheat your oven to 180°C (355°F). Remove the pork from the fridge at least 15-30 minutes before cooking. Remove the cling film, put the pork on a baking tray and scatter the curry leaves and onion slices over the meat. Cover tightly with foil and bake in the oven for 1½ hours.

Remove the tray from the oven, turn the pork over and continue to bake, uncovered, for another 1-1¼ hours, basting two to three times in the last half hour. Crank up the heat to 200°C (395°F) in the last 5 minutes. If the pan dries out, add 4-5 tablespoons of water to the dish. Cook until the pork is really tender, enough to fork apart. Rest for 10 minutes prior to serving.

Pork Belly and Smoked-Bacon Ragu

SERVES 8

Pork belly + bacon = ragu! The fats from the pork belly adds immense amounts of flavour to this ragu. For this dish, select a piece of pork belly that has more meat than fat. If you need to slice off the skin, trim it well and create crackling out of it. Sprinkle that over the ragu when serving for added indulgence!

750 g (1.6 lbs) skinless pork belly, cut into 3-cm (1.2-in) strips
1 large onion (220 g, 7.5 oz), skin removed, finely diced
8 cloves garlic, crushed, skin discarded, finely chopped
250 g (8.8 oz) smoky bacon rashes, rind removed and discarded, cut into batons
1 teaspoon cracked black pepper
1 teaspoon dried chilli flakes
1 teaspoon smoked paprika
½ teaspoon ground cinnamon
½ teaspoon fennel seeds, toasted and ground
1 teaspoon dried oregano
2 tins tomato, 400 g (14 oz) each
250 ml (1 cup) white wine
1 teaspoon raw sugar
Parmesan rinds (optional)
Olive oil

500 g (1.1 lb) rigatoni pasta
Grated or shaved fresh parmesan
¼ cup parsley, chopped

In a large, heavy-based saucepan, heat 2-3 tablespoons of olive oil. Fry the chopped onion and garlic until lightly golden, add the bacon and cook until crisp and golden. Push all the bacon and onion mix to one side of the pan, then sear the pork belly until nicely caramelised.

Toss in the pepper, chilli flakes, paprika, cinnamon, ground fennel and oregano. Deglaze with the white wine, then add the tomatoes. Stir in the sugar, add the parmesan rind, if using. Cover and cook for 1½-2 hours on low heat until the meat is super tender and breaks away easily.

I like serving this with rigatoni because the large barrels catch plenty of the incredibly meaty sauce. Cook the pasta in lots of lightly salted water according to the packet instructions until al dente. Place a large sauce pan over high heat. Drain the pasta and add to the pan. Spoon in ladles of sauce as desired. Toss until well combined. Remove and serve immediately with extra parmesan shavings and chopped parsley.

Note: I usually freeze the ends of my parmesan cheese. Next time you go through a wedge of fresh parmesan, don't throw out the rind, they come in very handy in flavouring dishes.

Pork Neck Roasted in Fermented Chilli Bean Paste

SERVES 4

Slow-cooking pork neck makes it super tender! The fermented chilli bean paste gives this dish a certain spicy richness that goes perfectly with noodles or simply steamed rice.

1.5 kg (3.3 lbs) pork neck, halved lengthways, fat trimmed

MARINADE
1 tablespoon soy sauce
4 tablespoons hoisin sauce
3 rounded tablespoons dou ban jiang (fermented chilli bean sauce)
2 teaspoons raw sugar

6 cloves garlic, crushed, skin discarded
25 g (0.9 oz) ginger, peeled, sliced
1 large red onion, peeled, halved, cut into wedges
4 dried red chillies
1 star anise
1 cinnamon stick
2 teaspoons Szechuan peppercorns, toasted
2 large stalks spring onions, sliced to 6-cm (2.4-in) lengths
3½ tablespoons Shaoxing wine
500 ml (2 cups) chicken stock
Oil

Preheat your oven to 170°C (338°F).

Mix the soy sauce, hoisin sauce, fermented chilli bean sauce and raw sugar in a bowl. Stir well and set aside.

Heat 2 tablespoons of oil in a Dutch oven or heavy-based pan over medium-high heat. Sear the pork neck all over until nicely brown and lightly charred at the edges. Remove and set aside.

In the same pan, fry the garlic, ginger, onions, dried chillies, star anise, cinnamon, Szechuan peppercorns and spring onions for a couple of minutes or until fragrant. Deglaze the pan with Shaoxing Chinese wine, then add the marinade. Stir well. Return the pork to the pan and toss to coat.

Pour in the chicken stock, cover, and bake in the oven for 2½ hours or until tender. Add ¼ cup of water at a time if the sauce becomes too dry.

Remove from the oven and rest the pork for 10 minutes. To serve, slice each piece of pork into 1-cm (0.4-in) medallions or fork apart, then pour over the sauce with all the lovely, gooey bits.

Note: I like to use a Dutch oven (cast iron Le Creuset or equivalent) to cook these half roast, half braise dishes as they conduct heat incredibly well. If you don't have one, don't worry, just do all the searing and cooking in a pan, then transfer into a baking dish and bake. Remember to cover the dish with foil and prick a few holes in it to let some of the steam escape.

Slow-Baked Satay Pork

SERVES 4-6

This is a really delicious dish that doesn't require you to slave over the stove for hours. It's very easy to prepare and the result looks like you've put in way more effort than you actually have! Give it a go!

750 g (1.6 lbs) whole pork neck
    or boneless shoulder

SPICE PASTE
3 cloves garlic, crushed, skin
    discarded
1 large (150 g, 5.3 oz)
    Spanish red onion, peeled,
    roughly chopped
1 large red hot chilli, roughly
    chopped
1 large stalk lemongrass, white
    root-end only, roughly
    chopped
½ teaspoon belacan
    (shrimp paste)
2 teaspoons ground coriander
1 teaspoon ground cumin
1 teaspoon ground turmeric
2 teaspoons sugar
1 teaspoon salt
1 tablespoon cold-pressed,
    extra-virgin coconut oil
180 ml (¾ cup) coconut milk
2 tablespoons kecap manis
    (Indonesian sweet soy sauce)

To make the spice paste, place the garlic, onion, chilli, lemongrass and shrimp paste in a food processor and blend until a smooth paste forms. Add the coriander, cumin, turmeric, sugar and salt and blitz to combine. Pour into a glass or ceramic bowl, then mix in the coconut oil, followed by half cup of the coconut milk and the kecap manis.

Place the pork in a baking dish just a little larger than the pork pieces, pour over the marinade and turn over a few times to coat thoroughly. Cover with cling film and marinate the pork overnight in the fridge.

When you are ready to cook, preheat your oven to 200°C (395°F).

Remove the cling film and cover the baking dish tightly with foil, then bake for 20 minutes. Reduce the temperature to 170°C (338°F) and continue cooking for another 1½ hours.

Remove from the oven and pour the remaining coconut milk over the meat. Cover with foil and return to the oven to bake for another hour until the meat is tender and shreds apart easily.

Serve this shredded as part of a shared-meal banquet with lightly pickled cucumber and rice.

Note: This spice paste is brilliant with chicken as well. Butterfly a whole chicken, marinate and roast flat.

Grilled Gochujang Pork

SERVES 4

Gochujang has a permanent spot in my fridge now. It's a Korean fermented hot pepper paste that is both sweet and savoury. It goes well with anything and everything from seafood to meats and works wonders with pork.

500 g (1.1 lbs) pork tenderloin, patted dry with paper towels, sinew removed, sliced into 1-cm (0.4-in) pieces
Oil
Sesame seeds, toasted

MARINADE
10 g (0.4 oz) ginger, grated
3 cloves garlic, peeled, grated
2 stalks spring onions, finely chopped, keep aside 1 tablespoon
3 teaspoons soy sauce
2 teaspoons mirin
2 teaspoons gochujang (Korean hot pepper paste)
2 teaspoons hoisin sauce
1 teaspoon sesame oil
1 teaspoon honey
½ teaspoon freshly ground pepper

In a large glass bowl, mix the marinade ingredients. Remember to leave 1 tablespoon of the chopped spring onions aside. Put in the sliced pork, toss well, cover with cling film and leave in the fridge to marinate for a few hours.

Remove from the fridge about 10 minutes prior to cooking. Heat a large fry pan with about 2 tablespoons of oil over high heat. Add the pork slices and sear until just cooked.

Plate, then sprinkle over the toasted sesame seeds and the reserved tablespoon of finely chopped spring onions.

Note: The pork may be chargrilled for that extra-smoky flavour.

Spiced Pork Open-Faced Sandwich

SERVES 4

If you weren't born in or spent your childhood in Singapore then an open-faced spicy, meaty sandwich will be a foreign concept to you. But trust me, try it and you will love it. This is inspired by Roti John, literally John's Bread, which uses chicken or mutton. The dish was said to be invented by a Malay hawker for a British soldier named John!

1½ cups shredded masala-spiced roasted pork shoulder (page 53)

1 sourdough baguette, cut into quarters each about 13 cm (5 in) in length, then halve each lengthways without slicing through

4 eggs

1 large onion, peeled, halved, finely sliced

2 green chillies, finely sliced

2 teaspoons curry powder

½ teaspoon smoked paprika

Sea salt

Oil

Butter

Fresh coriander

Sriracha chilli sauce

Whisk the eggs in a bowl. Add the onions, chillies, curry powder, paprika, a good pinch of salt and stir to combine. Toss in the shredded cooked pork. Divide this into four portions.

Heat 2 tablespoons of oil and a knob of butter in a large-surfaced, non-stick pan over medium-high heat.

Pour one portion of the spiced egg, onion and meat mixture onto the centre of the pan. Place a set of the baguette cut side facing down on top of the mixture and press down gently. Cook until the egg starts to brown, then close the sandwich and toast each side until crisp. Repeat with the remaining ingredients. You may have to clean the surface of the pan before cooking up the next batch.

To serve, slice each piece into quarters, scatter over some fresh coriander leaves and drizzle with Sriracha chilli sauce.

Ngo Hiang

Deep-fried Chinese meat rolls

MAKES 10-12 ROLLS

I have eaten Ngo Hiang from as far back as I can remember – and it definitely deserves a spot on the dinner table whether for the family or guests.

FILLING
500 g (1.1 lbs) minced veal and pork mince, minced pork or minced chicken
350 g (12.3 oz) raw prawns, peeled, deveined, roughly chopped
150 g (5.3 oz) peeled or tinned water chestnuts, chopped
30 g (1 oz) dried shiitake mushrooms, soaked in water for a few hours to rehydrate, chopped
1 onion (100 g, 3.5 oz), finely diced
1 carrot (150 g, 5.3 oz), grated
2 cloves garlic, peeled, finely chopped
3 stalks spring onions, finely chopped
1 egg, lightly beaten
2 tablespoons soy sauce
2 teaspoons white pepper
2 teaspoons five-spice powder
1 tablespoon tapioca flour

1 packet (125 g, 4.4 oz) dried beancurd sheets/skins
Tapioca flour for dusting
Oil for shallow frying
Kecap manis (Indonesian sweet soy sauce) for dipping

CHILLI SAUCE
100 g (3.5 oz) large red hot chillies, roughly chopped
Zest and juice of ½ a lime or 3-4 kalamansi limes
1½ teaspoons brown sugar
2 tablespoons sweet chilli sauce

To make the chilli sauce, place all its ingredients in a food processor and blend till combined.

Place all the filling ingredients together in a bowl and mix well. Divide the mixture into 10-12 portions or more, depending on the size and number of rolls you wish to make.

Cut each beancurd sheet into 20-cm (8-in) squares, or smaller as you wish. Wipe them down with a slightly damp kitchen towel. Lightly dust the top half of each sheet with tapioca flour.

Place a portion of filling lengthways at a third of the sheet closest to you, leaving space on either side. Cover the filling with the bottom part of the sheet and fold in the sides. Roll to make a sausage-like parcel. Alternatively roll into a sausage-like parcel and secure either ends with toothpicks or string.

To steam the rolls, place them on a lightly oiled steamer tray or a flat plate, then steam the rolls for about 8-10 minutes. Remove from the steamer and discard any liquid. Pat dry the rolls.

Pour 2.5 cm (1 in) deep of oil into a large fry pan and place over medium to high heat. Fry the rolls a couple at a time on all sides until they are nicely brown and crispy. Drain on paper towels.

You may skip the steaming process and deep-fry the rolls raw. In that case, it will take about 10-12 minutes to get them brown and crisp. You will also need to manage the heat by lowering and increasing as necessary.

Slice each roll on the diagonal into bite-sized pieces and serve with the chilli sauce and some kecap manis (Indonesian sweet soy sauce).

Lamb-Shank Rendang

SERVES 4

If you're a lamb lover, this is a must! It is as good as the original beef version! Shanks are relatively inexpensive. Cooked well, they are tender, juicy and full of flavour. Rendang is usually better made a day or two ahead so that the flavours have time to develop.

1.5 kg (3.3 lbs) lamb shank, excess fat trimmed
1 teaspoon cumin seeds, toasted, ground
1 teaspoon fennel seeds, toasted, ground
1–2 teaspoons hot paprika to taste
2½ tablespoons coriander seeds, toasted, ground
1 litre (4 cups) coconut milk
75 g (¾ cup) freshly grated coconut or desiccated coconut
2–3 teaspoons raw sugar to taste
2 teaspoons salt or to taste
Oil

SPICE PASTE
25 large dried red chillies (about 25 g, 0.9 oz), soaked in hot water until softened, drained
2 large fresh red chillies, roughly chopped
3 cloves garlic, crushed, skin discarded
2 large onions (about 330 g, 11.5 oz), peeled, roughly chopped
15 g (0.5 oz) ginger, peeled, roughly chopped
15 g (0.5 oz) galangal, roughly chopped
15 g (0.5 oz) turmeric, roughly chopped
4 large stalks lemongrass, white root-ends only, roughly chopped, bruise the stalk and retain

Place the lamb shanks in a large pot, cover with water and bring to the boil. Let it boil for about 20 minutes, skimming off all the scum and fat that rises to the top. Drain.

In the meantime, place the dried chillies, fresh red chillies, garlic, onions, ginger, galangal, turmeric and chopped lemongrass in a blender or food processor and blend to a fine paste.

In a separate saucepan large enough to hold all the shanks, heat 4 tablespoons of oil over medium heat, then pour in the paste and fry for about 8 minutes until fragrant.

Add the ground cumin, fennel, paprika and coriander and fry for a further 2 minutes. Gently pour in the coconut milk and 250 ml (1 cup) of water, stirring to loosen and blend in the spice paste.

Add the shanks along with the reserved lemongrass stalks and stir well to coat. Lower the heat to a simmer, cover and cook for 2½–3 hours, stirring every 30 minutes to make sure the bottom doesn't burn. If the spice paste gets too thick, add 4 tablespoons of water at a time.

While the shanks are cooking, prepare the kerisik (toasted coconut). Toast the grated coconut in a dry pan over medium heat until deep golden and nicely toasted. Take it as far as you can without burning it; a rich amber would be brilliant! This will not only give your rendang its classic, rich flavour but also provide good colour.

After about 2 hours of cooking the shanks, add the kerisik to the pot of lamb shank along with the sugar and salt and cook until the shanks are super tender, able to fall off the bones but still holding its shape. This could take from 30–60 minutes. Serve hot!

Indian Slow-Roasted Spiced Lamb

SERVES 4-6

I grew up not eating a lot of lamb and disliked its strong scent. Living in Australia with friends who have cooked beautiful lamb for me has changed my view. The key is to marinate and cook the lamb well. This recipe has the flavours of Indian spices that works well with lamb. It's an easy dish for a big dinner.

1.5 kg (3.3 lbs) boneless, flat lamb shoulder or boneless, butterflied lamb leg, trimmed

MARINADE
6 cloves garlic, skin removed, coarsely grated
20 g (0.7 oz) ginger, peeled, coarsely grated
3 large green or red hot chillies, halved, thinly sliced on the diagonal
1 large (about 200 g, 7 oz) Spanish onion, peeled, halved and thinly sliced
2 stalks curry leaves
⅓ cup loosely packed coriander root and stems
¼ teaspoon ground cinnamon
¼ teaspoon sumac
¼ teaspoon ground turmeric
¼ teaspoon ground fennel
1 teaspoon ground coriander
1 teaspoon ground cumin
1 teaspoon chilli powder or chilli flakes
6 green cardamon pods, crushed, seeds removed and ground
1 star anise
5 cloves
1 cinnamon stick, broken into 4 pieces
Zest of 1 large Tahitian lime or 2-3 small limes
2 tablespoons pomegranate molasses
2 tablespoons grape or date molasses
2 teaspoons smoked sea salt
2 teaspoons raw sugar
1 tablespoon olive oil

Trim the excess fats from the lamb, leaving some intact. This will help flavour the meat and keep it moist. Dry the meat with paper towels and score both sides with a sharp knife.

Mix all the marinade ingredients in a glass or ceramic bowl. Rub and massage the marinade all over the meat. Leave to marinate in the refrigerator overnight.

Remove the lamb from the refrigerator and leave at room temperature for about an hour. Preheat your oven to 150°C (300°F). Place the lamb and all the marinade in a foil-lined roasting dish. Pour in 250 ml (1 cup) of water, cover tightly with foil and cook in the oven for 2½-3 hours or until tender.

Increase the heat to 200°C (390°F) degrees, remove the foil and flip the lamb over. Bake for a further 30 minutes until the surface is slightly charred and the meat is super tender.

Remove from the oven, loosely cover with foil and rest for 15 minutes.

Slice or simply shred. Serve with my Spiced Rice (page 126) or Spiced Buttered Couscous (page 119) and Cumin Yoghurt Dressing (page 156).

Teppanyaki

Japanese Hot Plate

SERVES 8

Teppanyaki or Japanese hot plate, is one of the best dining experiences along with a good steamboat feast (page 70). We have teppanyaki quite often at home when entertaining friends. It's a social event in itself, incredibly fun and best of all, the kids love it! All the preparation is done in advance so you, as the cook, can enjoy cooking up this feast with those around the table. All you need to do is pick up a teppanyaki hotplate from your local Asian supermarket, set it up in the middle of your dining table, scatter bowls of different ingredients around the table along with the accompaniments. Diners bring their biggest appetite and enjoy the feast!

BEEF

300 g (10.5 oz) rump, sirloin or tenderloin, sliced thinly across the grain
1 tablespoon oyster sauce
1 tablespoon soy sauce
1 tablespoon Shaoxing wine
1 teaspoon sesame oil
½ teaspoon white pepper
5 g (0.2 oz) young ginger, coarsely grated
½ teaspoon Szechuan peppercorns, toasted and ground

CHICKEN

300 g (10.5 oz) chicken breast, sliced thinly across the grain
1 teaspoon hoisin sauce
1 teaspoon soy sauce
1 teaspoon mirin
1 teaspoon gochujang (Korean hot pepper paste)
1 teaspoon sesame oil
½ teaspoon white pepper
5 g (0.2 oz) young ginger, peeled, coarsely grated
½ teaspoon raw sugar

PORK

300 g (10.5 oz) pork tenderloin, sliced across the grain
1 tablespoon soy sauce
1 tablespoon mirin
10 g (0.4 oz) young ginger, peeled, coarsely grated
1 spring onion, finely sliced
1 teaspoon sesame oil
½ teaspoon white pepper
½ teaspoon raw sugar

PRAWNS

500 g (1.1 lbs) fresh king or tiger prawns, peeled, deveined
1 red chilli, finely diced
2 cloves garlic, finely chopped
1 tablespoon finely chopped coriander stem and root
1 tablespoon finely chopped spring onion
5 g (0.2 oz) young ginger, peeled, finely julienned
Good pinch of sea salt
Freshly cracked black pepper

FISH

300 g (10.5 oz) white fish, finely sliced
1 red chilli, finely sliced
½ teaspoon white pepper
1 teaspoon Shaoxing wine
1 teaspoon soy sauce
1 teaspoon sesame oil
5 g (0.2 oz) young ginger, peeled, finely julienned
1 spring onion, sliced thinly on the diagonal

SQUID

1 small whole squid (about 600 g, 1.3 lbs)
1 large red chilli, finely sliced on the diagonal
1 large clove garlic, peeled, finely julienned
5 g (0.2 oz) young ginger, peeled, finely julienned
1 tablespoon finely chopped coriander stem and root
1 lemongrass, white root-end only, blanched in boiling water for 30 seconds, then very finely sliced on the diagonal
1½ teaspoons fish sauce
½ teaspoon raw sugar
Good pinch of sea salt

MUSHROOMS
400 g (14 oz) assorted fresh
    mushrooms (king brown,
    shimeji, enoki)

CHILLI HONEY MISO SAUCE
30 g (1 oz) miso
30 g (1 oz) gochujang
    (Korean Hot Pepper Paste)
1 tablespoon honey
1 tablespoon mirin

DARK SOY AND BLACK VINEGAR
DRESSING
1 tablespoon dark soy sauce
2 tablespoons black vinegar
1 tablespoon soy sauce
1 tablespoon water
1 teaspoon sesame oil
1 teaspoon chilli oil
2 teaspoons raw sugar
¼ teaspoon freshly ground
    Szechuan pepper
1 red chilli, finely chopped
1 heaped tablespoon finely
    chopped coriander stems and
    roots
1 heaped tablespoon finely
    chopped spring onion

PEANUT SAUCE
    (page 132)

ACCOMPANIMENTS
150 g (5.3 oz) kim chi
    (store bought)
Bean sprouts, chilli, herb salad
    (page 113)
Stir-fried shredded greens
    (page 110)
Lettuce leaves
Steamed rice

Marinate the beef, chicken, pork, prawns and fish by mixing each with their respective marinade in a non-reactive, glass or ceramic bowl. Cover with cling film and keep them chilled until ready to use. You can prepare this a day ahead, just add the ginger, if the recipe calls for it, on the day of serving.

To prepare the squid, clean it by pulling out the tentacles. Remove the cartilage and all entrails from the inside the body. Peel off the purplish membrane from the body too. Cut off the wings then slice open the squid into a single flat piece. Scrape off any remaining visible muck. Rinse the tentacles, wings and body, then slice into bite-sized pieces of 5 x 2 cm (2 x 0.8 in). Mix in a bowl with the marinade.

Prepare the sauces by mixing each set of ingredients in separate bowls. This can also be made a day ahead.

Cook 3-4 cups of rice and keep warm.

Prepare the side dishes and place them in serving bowls.

Just before you are ready to serve, add 1½ tablespoons of neutral flavoured oil (rice bran, vegetable, grapeseed) into each bowl of raw ingredients. Preheat the hotplate to medium-high setting and start cooking! Manage the temperature as you go along. One rule of thumb: don't overcrowd the hotplate.

Table setting: Each diner should have a bowl of rice and a side plate, a pair of chopsticks, a spoon and a napkin. Place small tongs or chopsticks around the table to handle the raw food.

Steamboat

SERVES 8-10

Steamboat was a very common meal at home in my early childhood days. Mom would lightly marinate the meats and thread them through individual skewers in the Satay Celup style. It was fun for us to eat this way! At the end of the meal, my brother and I would compare who ate more by counting how many skewers we each had. The pièce de résistance was the incredibly rich and flavoursome broth left for us to toss in some noodles and slurp! It gave a feeling of sheer satisfaction, jubilation and pure happiness.

If you aren't up to slogging through threading the meats onto skewers, simply use tongs or chopsticks to drop the meats into the simmering broth, then fish them out with mini wire-basket ladles. If you don't have a steamboat, a deep electric pan will suffice. Then again buying a proper steamboat is an investment worth your while!

The following items make a pretty fancy affair, so pick and choose, and add or replace what you like. Also feel free to change the flavours of the broth but keep it light and make sure the marinades match well. You can also pull back on the marinades, enrich the broth and create more dipping sauces. Let your creative juices run wild!

BEEF
300 g (10.5 oz) sirloin or tenderloin, sliced very thinly across the grain
1 tablespoon oyster sauce
1 tablespoon soy sauce
1 tablespoon Shaoxing wine
1 teaspoon sesame oil
½ teaspoon white pepper
5 g (0.2 oz) young ginger, coarsely grated

CHICKEN
300 g (10.5 oz) chicken breast, sliced thinly across the grain
1 teaspoon hoisin sauce
1 teaspoon soy sauce
1 teaspoon mirin
1 teaspoon sesame oil
½ teaspoon white pepper
5 g (0.2 oz) young ginger, peeled, coarsely grated
½ teaspoon raw sugar

PORK
300 g (10.5 oz) pork tenderloin, sliced thinly across the grain
1 tablespoon hoisin sauce
1 tablespoon soy sauce
1 tablespoon Shaoxing wine
10 g (0.4 oz) young ginger, peeled, coarsely grated
1 teaspoon sesame oil
½ teaspoon white pepper
½ teaspoon raw sugar

PRAWNS
500 g (1.1 lbs) king or tiger prawns, peeled, deveined
1 bunch fresh coriander, finely chopped
2 cloves garlic, grated
1 small spring onion, finely chopped
5 g (0.2 oz) young ginger, peeled, grated
Good pinch of sea salt

FISH
300 g (10.5 oz) white fish, finely sliced
½ teaspoon freshly cracked black pepper
1 tablespoon Shaoxing wine
1 stalk spring onion, finely chopped
5 g (0.2 oz) young ginger, peeled, finely julienned

SQUID
1 kg whole squid (2.2 lbs)
1 large red chilli, finely sliced on the diagonal
2 cloves garlic, peeled, grated
10 g (0.4 oz) young ginger, peeled, grated
1 tablespoon finely chopped fresh coriander
2 teaspoons fish sauce
½ teaspoon raw sugar
Good pinch of salt

500 g (1.1 lbs) mussels, cleaned

VEGETABLES
1 bunch choy sum or bok choy, quartered
1 bunch fresh mustard greens, halved lengthwise
500 g (1.1 lbs) assorted fresh mushrooms (woodear fungus, shimeji, pearl, oyster, enoki)

TOFU
400 g (14 oz) fresh tofu, cut into 2-cm (0.8-in) cubes
200 g (7 oz) tofu puffs

NOODLES

120 g (4.2 oz) dried bean thread vermicelli, soaked in water to soften, drained

300 g (10.5 oz) Hokkien yellow noodles, blanched quickly in boiling water, drained

STOCK

3 litres (12.5 cups) good quality chicken stock or vegetable stock

10 slices ginger

10 cloves garlic, crushed

5 large spring onions, trimmed, sliced into 10-cm (4-in) lengths

10 dried shiitake mushrooms

Cracked black pepper

Steamed Jasmine rice from 3-4 cups raw rice

CHILLI SAUCE

200 g (7 oz) large red hot chillies, roughly chopped

Zest and juice of 1 lime or 6-8 calamansi limes

3 teaspoons brown sugar

4 tablespoons sweet chilli sauce

DARK SOY AND BLACK VINEGAR DRESSING

1 tablespoon dark soy sauce

2 tablespoons black vinegar

1 tablespoon light soy sauce

1 tablespoon chicken or vegetable stock

1 teaspoon sesame oil

1 teaspoon chilli oil

2 teaspoons raw sugar

¼ teaspoon freshly ground Szechuan pepper

1 red chilli, finely chopped

1 heaped tablespoon finely chopped coriander stem and root

1 heaped tablespoon finely chopped spring onion

Marinate the beef, chicken, pork, prawns and fish by mixing each with their respective marinades in a non-reactive, glass or ceramic bowl. Cover with cling film and keep them chilled until ready to use. You can prepare this a day ahead, just add the ginger on the day of serving.

To prepare the squid, clean it by pulling out the tentacles. Remove the cartilage and all entrails from the inside the body. and peel off the purplish membrane from the body too. Cut off the wings then slice open the squid into a single flat piece. Scrape off any remaining visible muck. Rinse the tentacles, wings and body, then slice into bite-sized pieces of 5 x 2 cm (2 x 0.8 in). Mix in a bowl with the marinade.

Prepare the sauces by mixing each set of ingredients in separate bowls. For the chilli sauce, place all the ingredients in a food processor and blend till combined. Set aside. These can also be made a day ahead. I tend to make extra batches of each sauce.

To make the cooking stock, place the chicken or vegetable stock along with all the ingredients into a large saucepan and bring to a boil, lower the heat and simmer for 15 minutes. Remove from the heat and set aside to infuse.

Cook 3-4 cups of rice and keep warm.

Prepare the side dishes and place them in serving bowls.

Just before your guests arrive, pour 2 litres (8.5 cups) of the prepared stock into your steamboat or pot, cover and bring to the boil, then lower to a simmer. Keep the remainder of the stock aside for topping up.

Arrange a serving of each dish, along with the dipping sauces, on both sides of the table. Guests can start cooking anything they like by submerging the raw ingredients into the steamboat until cooked then dipping them into the sauces.

Table setting: Each diner should have a bowl of rice and a side plate, a pair of chopsticks, a spoon and a napkin. Get mini wire-basket ladles if available. Reserve a set of extra bowls for the soup. Place small tongs or chopsticks around the table to handle the raw food.

Grilled Miso Cod

SERVES 4

This is my take on a Nobu classic! It's simple, delicious and so easy to cook. The perilla leaves, also called Japanese shiso leaves, imparts a beautiful flavour to the dish.

4 cod fillets (150 g, 5.3 oz each)
4 tablespoons white wine
1 tablespoon soy sauce
4 levelled tablespoons white
   miso paste
1 tablespoon sugar
2 tablespoons oil

ACCOMPANIMENTS
150 g (5.3 oz) white cabbage,
   very finely shredded
4-8 large Shiso leaves
1 cup pickled vegetables
   (page 157)

Mix the white wine, soy sauce, miso and sugar together in a glass bowl. Stir well. Add 1-2 tablespoons of water to dilute the marinade. Taste and add more sugar if you wish.

Pat the fish fillets dry with paper towels then rub the manrinade all over the fish. Set aside.

Preheat the broiler or grill of your oven to 220°C (395°F). Rub 2 tablespoons of oil all over the cod and bake in the oven skin-side up for 8-10 minutes, according to the size of the fish, until just cooked and the edges are lightly charred.

Toss the shredded cabbage in olive oil with a pinch of sugar and a squeeze of lemon juice. Place each fish on 2 shiso leaves and serve with the shredded cabbage salad and pickled vegetables.

Pan-Fried Pomfret with Shredded Ginger

SERVES 4

Here is a simple but delicious dish, one that my mom used to cook a lot of when I was growing up. It's great for both family meals and as part of a banquet!

Whole pomfret (about 750 g,
   1.6 lbs), gutted and cleaned
1-2 teaspoons soy sauce, to taste
1 teaspoon Shaoxing wine
White pepper
30 g (1 oz) young ginger,
   peeled, julienned
1 stalk spring onions, sliced
   thinly on the diagonal
¼ lemon
Oil

To prepare the fish, clean and pat dry with paper towels. Score the fish diagonally on both sides. Rub the soy sauce, Shaoxing wine and white pepper all over the fish, including the cavity, and tuck most of the ginger into the scored bits leaving the remainder for the topping. Set aside.

Heat a large wok with about 3 tablespoons of oil over high heat. Gently lower the fish into the piping-hot wok. Cook for about 5 minutes or until crispy and golden, then turn over to cook the other side for a further 3-5 minutes. Once the fish is cooked through, remove and plate. Squeeze over some lemon juice and top with the reserved ginger and spring onions. Serve immediately.

Pan-Seared Barramundi with Pineapple and Mustard Seed Chutney

SERVES 4

I love the earthy flavour of barramundi. The texture is pretty similar to sea bass so, if you can't find a good barra when you hit the fish markets, pick up some seabass. This pineapple chutney has a subtle spice flavour. Select a ripe pineapple for added natural sweetness. I like the pineapple with a little bit of crunch but it's a matter of preference. Cook it for longer on a low flame if you like yours softer.

4 barramundi fillets (200 g, 7 oz each) patted dry with paper towels
Sea salt
Freshly cracked black pepper
Lemon wedge
1-2 Lebanese cucumber, sliced into ribbons
Olive oil

PINEAPPLE CHUTNEY
1 tablespoon olive oil
10 g (0.4 oz) ginger, peeled, finely julienned
1 small onion, peeled, halved and sliced
½ teaspoon black mustard seeds
½ teaspoon cumin seeds
1 stalk curry leaves
2 small dried chillies
200 g (7 oz) fresh ripe pineapple, cut into bite-sized wedges
4 strips fresh orange rind
20 g (0.7 oz) brown sugar
½ teaspoon salt
1 teaspoon apple cider vinegar
2 teaspoons lemon juice

Start by making the pineapple chutney. Heat 1 tablespoon of olive oil in a small saucepan over medium heat. Add the ginger and onions and cook until softened and lightly charred. Add the mustard seeds and wait for them to pop, then quickly toss in the cumin, curry leaves and dried chillies. Stir to combine.

Toss in the fresh pineapple chunks and orange rind, and allow to caramelise. Increase the heat, then add the sugar and salt, stirring until the sugar glazes and coats the pineapple. Deglaze with the vinegar and lemon juice. Reduce the heat, cover, and cook for a further 5 minutes or until the pineapple softens and yet remains a little crunchy. Cook for a while longer if you prefer softer pineapple.

Season the fish well with salt and pepper and a drizzle of olive oil.

Preheat your oven to 180°C (355°F).

Place a large oven-proof fry pan over high heat. Fry the fish skin side down, pressing down gently to keep the skin flat on the pan. Cook until the skin is crispy. Transfer to the oven, leaving skin side down and cook for 2-3 minutes until the fish is just cooked. Remove from the oven and transfer to a serving dish crispy skin side up. Squeeze over some lemon juice. Serve the fish with cucumber ribbons and pineapple chutney with a drizzle of olive oil.

Baked Trout with Herb and Black Rice Stuffing

SERVES 4

Just two words: insanely delicious.

2 whole trouts (450 g, 1 lb
  each), gutted and cleaned
Sea salt
Freshly ground black pepper,
Zest and juice of half a lime
Olive oil

RICE STUFFING
½ cup cooked black rice
2 tablespoons roughly chopped
  coriander stems and leaves
2 tablespoons chopped spring
  onions
1 tablespoon roughly chopped
  mint
1 tablespoon roughly chopped
  Thai basil
½ large hot red chilli, finely
  sliced
¼ Spanish red onion, peeled,
  finely sliced
2 kaffir lime leaves, finely
  julienned
200 g (7 oz) mix of cherry and
  grape tomatoes
2 tablespoons pine nuts, toasted
1 tablespoon dried goji berries
1-2 tablespoons freshly squeezed
  orange juice
Zest of 1 lime
Pinch of sea salt
Freshly cracked black pepper

Preheat your oven to 200°C (395°F). Prepare a baking dish or baking sheet lined with foil then topped with greaseproof paper.

Mix all the stuffing ingredients in a bowl.

Season the fish well inside and out with salt and pepper and zest of half a lime. Rub some olive oil all over the fish.

Place the fish on the lined baking tray. Stuff the cavity of each fish with the herb rice stuffing. Don't worry if some spills out of the belly. These bits will crisp up nicely.

Bake for 20 minutes or so, depending on the size of your fish, until the fish are just cooked.

Remove from the oven, rest for 5 minutes and transfer to a serving dish. Squeeze over the juice of the half wedge of lime and serve with a leafy salad or greens.

Note: Using greaseproof paper prevents the fish skin from sticking and makes it a lot easier to transfer to a serving dish.

Black Cod with Sambal Buah Keluak

SERVES 4

This dish was totally inspired by a Polish girl I met while filming as a guest judge on MasterChef Poland in Singapore. It was incredible that she explored and experimented with the use of buah keluak, an ingredient the Peranakans love and yet so foreign to many Singaporeans, what more the Polish.

Buah keluak is the nut of Pangium edule, *a tall tree native to the mangrove swamps of Indonesia and Papua New Guinea. These nuts are poisonous but become edible with fermentation. Nuts and the mashed kernels, which have been prepared for cooking, are available in the markets of Indonesia, Malaysia and Singapore.*

4 black cod fillets (150 g, 5.3 oz each)
2 pieces large banana leaves
1 red chilli, thinly sliced
Lime wedges
60 ml (¼ cup) oil
1 tablespoon tamarind pulp soaked in 3½ tablespoons water, rendered and sieved
½ teaspoon sea salt or to taste
1 teaspoon raw sugar or to taste

BUAH KELUAK SAMBAL
Flesh from 6 prepared buah keluak seeds (about 50-60 g prepared flesh)
2 cloves garlic, peeled, roughly chopped
1 small red Spanish onion or 4 red shallots, peeled, roughly chopped
4 large dried red chillies, soaked in hot water to soften
2 red chillies, roughly chopped
5 g (0.2 oz) galangal, roughly chopped
5 g (0.2 oz) fresh turmeric, roughly chopped
1 stalk lemongrass, white root-end only, roughly chopped
5 g (0.2 oz) belacan (shrimp paste, wrapped in foil and toasted on a dry pan
2 candlenuts
2 kaffir lime leaves

Make the buah keluak sambal by blending together the buah keluak flesh, garlic, onion, dried and fresh chillies, galangal, turmeric, lemongrass, shrimp paste, candlenuts and kaffir lime leaves until fine.

In a saucepan, heat 60 ml (¼ cup) of oil over medium heat. Add the sambal paste and cook until fragrant, about 8-10 minutes. Add 2 tablespoons of tamarind puree, 1 teaspoon of sugar and ½ teaspoon of salt or adjust to taste. Set aside to cool.

Coat each piece of fish with 1 tablespoon of buah keluak sambal, leave to marinade for an hour or overnight in the fridge.

Heat a non-stick fry pan on medium-high heat. Place a grill mesh over a separate flame on the stove. Pan sear the fish, skin side down, on the fry pan until crisp and golden. Put two layers of banana leaves on the open flame and place the fish skin side down on the leaves to cook till just done. The burnt banana leaves will impart a smoky falvour to the fish.

Alternatively, grill over the barbecue until the fish is cooked through or line a baking sheet with banana leaves, top with the fish and cook for 8-10 minutes (depending on the size of the fish) on the top grill of an oven preheated to 210°C (410°F). The fish should be just cooked with bits of the surface lightly charred.

Sprinkle over the sliced chillies, serve with lime wedges and any remaining sambal on the side as part of a shared meal.

Grilled Barramundi with Sambal Matah

SERVES 4

My travels to Bali opened a whole new world of sambals that are so different to the Singaporean style I grew up with. The Indonesians do it quite differently, and the Balinese, different yet again. It's fresh and super spicy, so adjust the amount of chillies (with or without seeds) in this recipe according to your taste.

600 g (1.3 lbs) barramundi or
  seabass fillet
6 cloves garlic, skin removed,
  finely grated
10 g (0.4 oz) ginger, skinned,
  finely grated
1½ teaspoons ground turmeric
2 teaspoons ground coriander
1 teaspoon sweet paprika
1 teaspoon sea salt
1 tablespoon (25 g) tamarind
  pulp, soaked in 4 tablespoons
  water, rendered and sieved
1 tablespoon cold-pressed, extra-
  virgin coconut oil
Large piece banana leaf

SAMBAL MATAH
4 tablespoons cold-pressed,
  extra-virgin coconut oil
1 small red Spanish onion,
  peeled, sliced very thinly
2 cloves garlic, crushed, skined,
  finely chopped
2-4 red chilli padi, to taste,
  thinly sliced into rings
2-4 green chilli padi, to taste,
  thinly sliced into rings
1 large red chilli, thinly sliced
  into rings
½ teaspoon belacan (shrimp
  paste), dry roasted, mashed
1 lemongrass stem, white root-
  end only, blanched then very
  finely chopped
4 kaffir lime leaves, finely sliced
Juice and zest of 1 lemon or lime
  or 4-5 kalamansi limes
2 teaspoons raw sugar
Pinch of salt

Mix the grated garlic, ginger, turmeric, coriander, paprika, salt and tamarind puree in a bowl. Rub the mixture all over the fish. Set aside to marinate for about 30 minutes.

Preheat your oven to 200°C (395°F).

Cut off the mid-rib of the banana leaf carefully, ensuring that there are no tears, then trim the leaf to fit your baking tray. Line the baking tray with foil, put the leaf on it, then place the fish, skin side down, on the leaf. Drizzle over the coconut oil and gather up the sides of the banana leaf and foil, leaving the fish exposed.

Place this in the oven under the grill and cook for approximately 10-12 minutes or until the fish is just cooked and a little charred. If you are cooking this over a barbecue, place the banana leaf fish parcel on the foil directly over high heat.

While the fish is cooking, prepare the sambal matah. Heat the coconut oil till hot and set aside. Mix all the remaining ingredients of the sambal matah and pour the hot coconut oil over it.

Once the fish is ready, serve immediately with the sambal matah and a wedge of lime.

Note: To dry roast the belacan, wrap it tightly in a single layer of foil and toast both sides on a dry pan for a few minutes. Alternatively, place in a preheated oven at 180°C (355°F) degrees for 10 minutes.

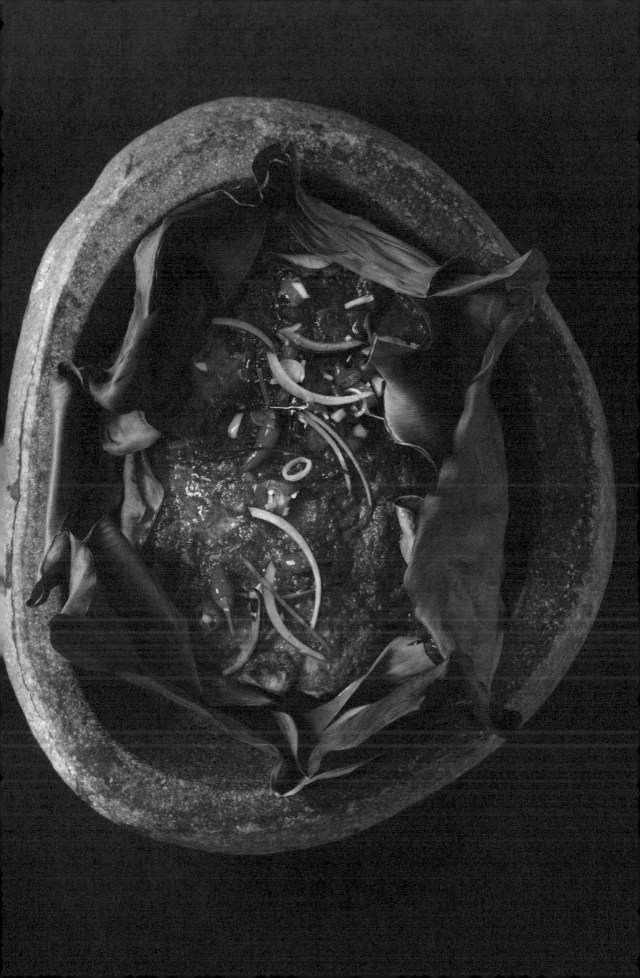

Mussels in Green Curry

SERVES 4

This might be the best alternative to Moules Marinières, the quintessential French dish. The most delicious thing about this dish for me is being able to scoop up the chillies, wilted leeks and coconut broth with empty mussel shells. The delicious, plump and juicy mussels are a bonus!

1 kg (2.2 lbs) mussels, cleaned, debearded, drained
1 medium leek, sliced diagonally
125 g (4.4 oz) green curry paste
1 large red chilli, sliced on the diagonal
1 stalk lemongrass, white root-end, bruised
250 ml (1 cup) coconut milk
1 teaspoon fish sauce
1 tablespoon shaved palm sugar
4 kaffir lime leaves
5 tablespoons olive oil
Extra lime juice

GREEN CURRY PASTE
1 teaspoon Thai gapi or belacan (shrimp paste)
¼ teaspoon coriander seeds, toasted
¼ teaspoon cumin seeds, toasted
¼ teaspoon white peppercorns, toasted
2-4 long hot green chillies according to taste, roughly chopped
4 green chillies, roughly chopped
2 stalks lemongrass, white root-end, roughly chopped
10 g (0.4 oz) galangal, roughly chopped
10 g (0.4 oz) turmeric, roughly chopped
1 medium Spanish onion or 10 shallots, peeled, roughly chopped
4 coriander roots, cleaned and roughly chopped
4 cloves garlic, peeled
Zest of 1 kaffir lime

Wrap the shrimp paste in foil and roast in the oven for 10 minutes or in a dry pan over low-medium heat for 5 minutes.

Blend it and all the other green curry paste ingredients into a fine paste.

In a large saucepan, heat about 4 tablespoons of olive oil on high heat. Add the leeks, chilli, lemongrass and cook for a couple of minutes until the leeks are wilted and lightly blistered. Add the green curry paste and cook for a couple of minutes. Deglaze with the coconut milk, stirring to remove all the sticky bits on the pan. Add the fish sauce and palm sugar. Toss in the mussels and finally scrunched-up kaffir lime leaves.

Mix the mussels with the sauce, cover and cook on high heat for 3-4 minutes until all the mussels are open. Remove from the heat, squeeze over some lime juice and serve immediately.

Note: If you are using a blender, it's difficult to make curry pastes in small quantities. This recipe makes more than the required amount. Store the remaining curry paste in a well-sealed jar or container and freeze.

Tamarind Chilli Crispy-Skin Salmon with Green Mango Herb Salad

SERVES 4

Tamarind and fish are a great combination. The tamarind chilli dressing is delicious but pungent with the addition of the shrimp paste, so use as little or as much as you desire. If you prefer it less sweet, pull back on the gula Melaka.

600 g (1.3 lbs) salmon fillets, cut into 4-cm (1.5-in) cubes, patted dry with paper towels
Sea salt
Fresh cracked black pepper
Crispy shallots
Oil

TAMARIND CHILLI DRESSING
5-10 g (0.2-0.4 oz) large dried red chillies (see note)
2 cloves garlic, peeled, minced in a mortar and pestle with a pinch of salt
5 g (0.2 oz) belacan (shrimp paste)
65 g (2.3 oz) gula Melaka, shaved
25 g (0.9 oz) tamarind pulp, soaked in 150 ml (³/₅ cup) hot water, rendered and sieved
1½ tablespoons lemon juice
2 large kaffir lime leaves, finely julienned

SALAD
½ telegraph cucumber or 1 Lebanese cucumber, unpeeled, shaved into ribbons
1 green mango, peeled, shaved into ribbons
1 small bunch coriander leaves
1 small bunch Thai basil leaves
2 wing beans, finely sliced
Squeeze of lemon juice
Pinch of sugar
Olive oil

Season the fish with salt and pepper and a drizzle of oil.

Place the soaked dried chillies and garlic in a food processor and blend until a fine paste.

Heat 2 tablespoons of oil in a small saucepan over medium heat, add the shrimp paste and mash with a wooden spatula. Cook for a minute until the shrimp paste becomes fragrant and starts to toast. Add the chilli garlic paste and continue to cook, stirring frequently, until fragrant.

Add the gula Melaka and cook until dark, glossy and sticky. Slowly pour in the tamarind puree. Cook until slightly thickened, then stir in the lemon juice and sprinkle on the kaffir lime leaves. Remove from heat and set aside.

Heat a non-stick fry pan over high heat. Place the fish pieces skin side down evenly around the pan and cook until crisp and golden. To ensure that the skin is evenly crispy, you may need to gently press with a spatula to keep the skin flat on the pan. Turn over, and cook the other side until three-quarter cooked. Pour over the tamarind chilli sauce and toss very gently to just coat. Be careful not to break up the fish pieces.

Combine the salad ingredients, and dress with lemon juice, sugar and olive oil just before serving.

Transfer the fish onto a serving plate along with all the sauce and top with the green mango, cucumber and herb salad. Sprinkle with crispy shallots and serve immediately.

Note: Adjust the quantity of the large, red dried chillies according to your taste. Also, leave the seeds in if you like the dish extra spicy, otherwise, deseed them. In any case, soak the chillies in hot water until softened before using them.

Fish with Coconut Green Masala in Banana Leaf

SERVES 4

This dish uses a double-cooking method. First, the coconut masala fish is wrapped into banana-leaf parcels and steamed. Then they are toasted over an open flame to produce a smoky and delicious flavour!

600 g (1.3 lbs) skinless white-fish fillet (barramundi, snapper, ling), cut into 4 equal pieces or left whole
4 tablespoons coconut cream
4 banana leaves, each large enough to wrap a piece of fish or 1 to wrap the whole fillet
1 red chilli, sliced
Sea salt

COCONUT GREEN MASALA
4 large green chillies, roughly chopped
2 green chillies (if you want more heat)
½ cup chopped fresh coriander, stems, roots and leaves
¼ cup chopped fresh mint leaves
2 cloves garlic, crushed, skin discarded
5 g (0.2) fresh turmeric
Zest of 1 lime or 5 calamansi limes
2 tablespoons lime juice
2 tablespoon coconut oil
½ teaspoon cumin seeds, toasted, coarsely ground
¼ teaspoon white pepper
100 g (3.5 oz) freshly grated coconut
¼ teaspoon sugar
¼ teaspoon sea salt

Prepare the steamer by bringing the water to a boil.

Place the chillies, coriander, mint, garlic, turmeric, lime zest and juice, coconut oil, cumin, pepper, coconut, sugar and salt in a blender and blitz to make a fine paste.

Place the banana leaves over the open flame of a stove to soften and release its oils. Allow to cool.

Divide the coconut masala into 4 portions. Smear half a portion in the middle of the banana leaf, place a piece of fish on it and top with the remaining half portion of masala. Spoon over 1 tablespoon of coconut cream, wrap snugly and tie securely with a string. Repeat with the remaining fish.

Place the parcels of fish in the steamer, ensuring that the openings are facing upwards to avoid any leakage. Steam for about 12–15 minutes. The fish is cooked when the flesh flakes away easily with a fork.

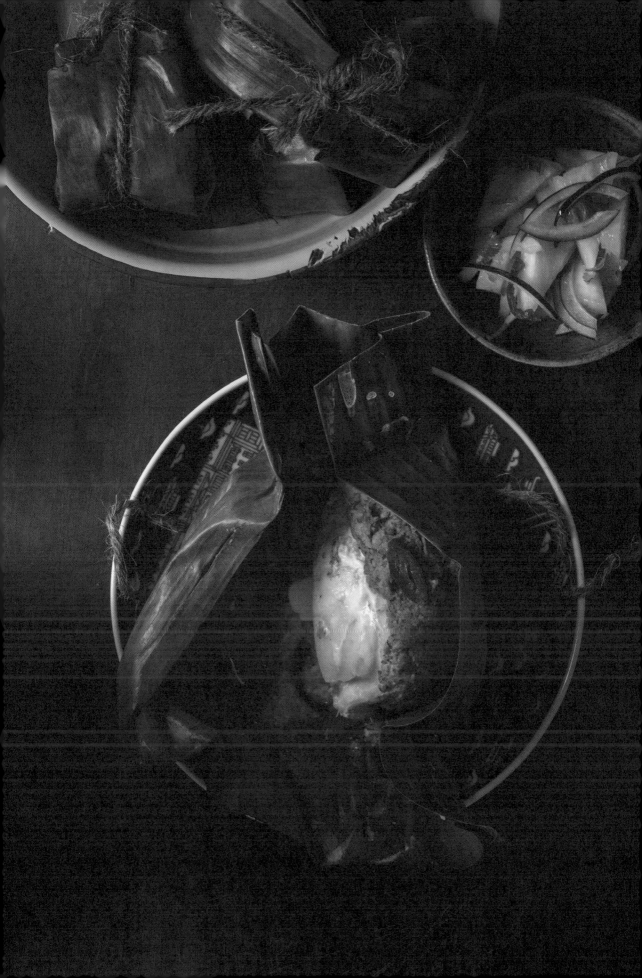

Chilli Prawns with Black Vinegar

SERVES 4

I love all the seafood recipes in this cookbook so much so it's really hard to pick a favourite. This one is exceptionally good. Salty, sweet and super spicy! Just make sure you pick up really fresh prawns.

750 g (1.6 lbs) whole prawns
Sea salt
Freshly cracked black pepper
1 teaspoon Szechuan peppercorns, toasted, coarsely ground
6 cloves garlic, peeled, chopped
15 g (0.5 oz) ginger, peeled, finely julienned
1-2 large red chillies, thinly sliced
2 tablespoons chopped fresh coriander root and stem
2 large stalks spring onions, chopped
1 cup fresh coriander leaves
Oil

SUACE
2 tablespoons Shaoxing wine
1 tablespoon chilli oil
2 tablespoons black vinegar
2 tablespoons kecap manis (Indonesian sweet soy sauce)
2 tablespoons Lao Gan Ma chilli sauce

Remove the heads and shells of the prawns but keep the tails intact. Set the prawns aside and keep the heads and shells to make prawn oil.

Run a sharp knife down the spine of the prawn to butterfly them. Remove the intestinal tracts. Marinate the prawns in a glass or ceramic bowl with sea salt, black pepper and Szechuan pepper. Set aside.

Make a sauce by mixing the Shaoxing wine chilli oil, black vinegar, kecap manis and chilli sauce in a small bowl.

Place a large fry pan or wok over high heat and add 2-3 tablespoons of oil. When the pan is hot and the oil is shimmering, add the garlic, ginger, chillies and chopped coriander. Stir and cook for a couple of minutes until they are slightly charred at the edges.

Add the prawns, discarding any liquid, and stir fry until almost cooked. Then add the sauce mixture and toss to combine. Top with spring onions and coriander leaves, toss, and serve immediately.

Note: I use made-in-China Lao Gan Ma brand chilli sauce for this dish. It's full of crispy onions, chillies and Szechuan peppers. For alternatives, look for chilli sauces that are cooked with dried crispy chilllies.

Fried Chillied Fish

SERVES 4

Here is a simple and quick double-fried fish dish which packs a good punch with the chilli heat. I love stir-fries that have chunky sauces. They almost serve as a vegetable in the dish. The fresh ginger, garlic, chillies, spring onions and coriander all add to the sauce which is great served with rice.

500 g (1.1 lbs) snapper or blue-eye cod fillets, sliced into bite-size pieces
½ teaspoon white pepper
½ teaspoon black pepper
½ teaspoon Szechuan pepper, toasted whole then ground with a mortar and pestle
½ teaspoon dried chilli flakes
½ teaspoon sea salt
75 g (½ cup) cornflour or tapioca flour
Vegetable or rice bran oil for deep-frying
2 tablespoons black vinegar
2 teaspoons soy sauce
2 tablespoons kecap manis (Indonesian sweet soy sauce)
2 teaspoons chilli oil
4 cloves garlic, finely chopped
20 g (0.7 oz) ginger, finely diced
2 heaped tablespoons finely chopped coriander stems and roots
2 large red hot chillies, finely diced
2 tablespoons Shaoxing wine
2 large stalks spring onions, finely chopped
½ cup roughly chopped fresh coriander leaves

Marinate the fish fillets with the white, black and Szechuan peppers, chilli flakes and salt.

Heat a medium-sized fry pan or wok filled with about 4 cm (1.5 in) of oil over high heat. While the oil is heating, toss the marinated fish with cornflour. Deep fry the fish in batches until the edges are slightly golden and crispy. Drain on paper towels.

Mix together the black vinegar, soy sauce, kecap manis and chilli oil. Set aside.

Remove all but 1 tablespoon of oil from the fry pan. Bring to high heat then fry the garlic, ginger, chopped coriander and chillies until blistered and golden. Deglaze with Shaoxing wine, then pour in the mixed sauce, Szechuan pepper and chilli flakes.

Allow the sauce to thicken slightly for 1–2 minutes, then add the fish, spring onions and coriander leaves. Toss to combine. Serve immediately with rice with other dishes.

Salmon, Kimchi and Herb Dumplings

MAKES ABOUT 60

One can never have too many dumpling recipes. These very sophisticated dumplings use a combination of a fatty fish like salmon with well fermented kimchi and loads of herbs. Chinkiang vinegar is a must-have dip for all dumplings!

60 wonton wrappers
Chilli oil
1 stalk spring onions, finely sliced
Crispy shallots

FILLING
400 g (14 oz) fresh skinless
    salmon, finely diced
50 g (1.8 oz) cabbage
4 cloves garlic, peeled, coarsely
    grated
20 g (0.7 oz) ginger, peeled,
    coarsely grated
2 large stalks spring onions,
    finely sliced
2 bunches fresh coriander, leaves,
    roots and stems roughly chopped
150 g (5.3 oz) kimchi, roughly
    chopped
3 teaspoons soy sauce
1 teaspoon sesame oil
1 teaspoon white pepper
2 teaspoons tapioca flour or
    cornflour

DRESSING
2 tablespoons soy sauce
2 tablespoons Chinkiang vinegar
1½ tablespoons kecap manis
    (Indonesian sweet soy sauce)
1 teaspoon sesame oil
2 teaspoons chilli oil
½ teaspoon dou ban jiang
    (chilli bean sauce)
½ teaspoon coarsely ground
    toasted Szechuan peppercorns
1 tablespoon finely sliced spring
    onion
1 tablespoon finely sliced fresh
    coriander

Finely shred the cabbage, microwave for 1 minute, then squeeze out as much of the moisture as possible between your palms. Chop finely.

Place all the ingredients for the filling in a large glass bowl and mix until well combined. I find it easiest to use a large fork to stir, followed by a spoon to finish off the mixing. This will ensure you don't compress and mush up the mixture too much.

For the dressing, mix all its ingredients in a glass jar. This can be made a few days in advance and stored in the fridge for up to a week or two.

To wrap a dumpling, place one teaspoon of the filling in the middle of a wonton wrapper. Dab the edges of half the wrapper with water, then fold the wrapper over the filling to make a triangle. Seal the dumpling by gently pressing outwards from the filling to the edges to ensure that there are no air pockets.

Hold the dumpling with the long side of the triangle away from you and bring the two sealed edges of the wrapper to the bottom. Secure by putting a tiny bit of water on one of the edges, overlap with the other, and pressing gently. Repeat with all the filling and wrappers.

Bring a medium to large saucepan of water to the boil. Poach the dumplings a bunch at a time, taking care not to overcrowd the saucepan. The dumplings will float when they are cooked.

Remove with a slotted spoon and place in individual bowls or a large plate. Sprinkle over the black vinegar chilli dressing and chilli oil then scatter over with chopped spring onions and crispy shallots.

Prawns Dumplings with Chinkiang Vinegar Chilli Dressing and XO Sauce

MAKES ABOUT 60

If I ever decide to open a restaurant, dumplings would feature prominently on the menu. There is something incredibly satisfying about making dumplings, and eating them is even more gratifying. So expect to find not just one dumpling recipe in this cookbook.

60 wonton wrappers

FILLING

300 g (10.5 oz) raw prawn meat, finely chopped

100 g (3.5 oz) white or savoy cabbage, finely shredded

1 medium carrot, finely shredded

1 cup chopped English spinach

2 large cloves garlic, peeled, coarsely grated

20 g (0.7 oz) ginger, peeled, coarsely grated

2 large stalks spring onions, finely chopped

2 heaped tablespoons finely chopped fresh coriander leaves and stems

2 tablespoons soy sauce

2 tablespoons mirin

1 teaspoon sesame oil

1 teaspoon freshly cracked white pepper

2 teaspoons tapioca flour or cornflour

DRESSING

2 tablespoons dark soy sauce

4 tablespoons Chinkiang black vinegar

2 tablespoons light soy sauce

2 tablespoons water

2 teaspoons sesame oil

2 teaspoons chilli oil

4 teaspoons raw sugar

¾ teaspoon freshly ground Szechuan pepper

1-2 large red chilli, finely diced

2 rounded tablespoons finely

Microwave the shredded the cabbage for 1 minute, then squeeze out as much of the moisture as possible between your palms. Do the same for the carrot and English spinach.

Place all the ingredients for the filling in a large glass bowl and mix until well combined. I find it easiest to use a large fork to stir, followed by a spoon to finish off the mixing. This will ensure you don't compress and mush up the mixture too much.

For the dressing, mix all its ingredients in a glass jar. This can be made a few days in advance and stored in the fridge for up to a week or two.

To wrap a dumpling, place one teaspoon of the filling in the middle of a wonton wrapper. Dab the edges of half the wrapper with water, then fold the wrapper over the filling to make a triangle. Seal the dumpling by gently pressing outwards from the filling to the edges to ensure that there are no air pockets.

Hold the dumpling with the long side of the triangle away from you and bring the two sealed edges of the wrapper to the bottom. Secure by putting a tiny bit of water on one of the edges, overlap with the other, and pressing gently. Repeat with all the filling and wrappers.

Bring a medium to large saucepan of water to the boil. Poach the dumplings a bunch at a time, taking care not to overcrowd the saucepan. The dumplings will float when they are cooked. Remove with a slotted spoon and place in individual bowls or a large plate. Sprinkle over the black vinegar chilli dressing, a dollop of my Black Bean XO Sauce (page 156) and scatter with chopped spring onions and crispy shallots.

sliced coriander stems and
roots
3-4 stalks spring onion, finely
sliced

TOPPING
Black Bean XO Sauce
(page 156)
1-2 stalks spring onions, finely
chopped
Crispy shallots

Steamed Barramundi with XO Sauce

SERVES 4

Everytime I cook this dish, I realize how much I love a good steamed fish. It's comforting and truly satisfying. Add the Black Bean XO Sauce and the dish is even better. Take the time to make a good XO sauce. Barramundi is a great fish to steam as it's tender and flaky. Feel free to use seabass as an alternative.

600 g (1.3 lbs) barramundi fillet
Freshly cracked white pepper
2 tablespoons Shoaxing wine
plus 1 teaspoon extra
20 g (0.7 oz) young ginger,
peeled, finely julienne
60 ml (¼ cup) good quality
vegetable stock
2 tablespoons soy sauce
1 teaspoon sesame oil
½ teaspoon raw sugar
3 tablespoons vegetable oil
3 large spring onions, finely
sliced on the diagonal
1-2 red chillies, finely sliced on
the diagonal (optional)
3 tablespoons Black Bean XO
Sauce (page 156)

Prepare the steamer by bringing the water to a boil.

Marinate the fish with cracked white pepper and rub the flesh with 1 teaspoon of Shaoxing wine. Place the fish on a plate skin side up, scatter the ginger on top and pour the vegetable stock around the fish. Steam the fish until just cooked, approximately 10-12 minutes depending on its size.

While the fish is steaming, mix the 2 tablespoons of Shaoxing wine, soy, sesame oil, sugar and 4 tablespoons of water in a small saucepan. Just before serving, bring this mixture to the boil then remove from the heat and set aside. In a small pan, heat the oil until shimmering.

As soon as the fish is cooked, remove from the steamer and pour away some of the liquid then pour the piping-hot oil over the fish. Now ladle on the sauce, top with spring onions, chilli and my Black Bean XO Sauce.

Note: When steaming, wrap the lid of the steamer with cloth to prevent moisture from dripping into the dish.

Jumbo Prawns and Mango Salad with Dried Shrimp "Dukkah"

SERVES 4

This is the perfect, fresh salad with large jumbo prawns to make during the sweet mango season. However, this recipe also works with tangy, green mangoes. The dried shrimp "dukkah" is delicious; lovely just over hot rice too!

4-6 jumbo prawns or 8 large prawns
2 stalks lemongrass, white root-ends only, bruised
Pinch of sea salt
2 tablespoons olive oil
½ -1 teaspoon sweet or hot paprika

DRIED SHRIMP "DUKKAH"
2 tablespoons medium-sized dried prawns, soaked for 2 hours, drained, pounded coarsely and fried till crispy
2 heaped tablespoons roasted salted peanuts, coarsely crushed
1 tablespoon white sesame seeds, toasted
1 tablespoon black sesame seeds, toasted
1 teaspoon dried chilli flakes
2 tablespoons crispy shallots, coarsely crushed
2 tablespoons garlic flakes, coarsely crushed
Sea salt to taste

MANGO SALAD
1 firm ripe mango, peeled, finely shredded
1 Lebanese cucumber, peeled, sliced on the diagonal, julienned
1 medium carrot, peeled, sliced on the diagonal, julienned
½ red capsicum, thinly sliced
2 red radishes, thinly sliced
1 small bunch watercress, washed, picked

Make the dressing by mixing all its ingredients until well combined. Set aside.

Fill a medium saucepan with water, add the lemongrass and salt, and bring to the boil. Reduce the heat to low and gently poach the prawns in this liquid until almost cooked, about 2 minutes. Remove and set aside to cool. When cool, peel the prawns, slice into half horizontally and remove the intestinal tracts.

To make the dried shrimp 'dukkah', ensure all ingredients are roughly chopped and crushed before mixing them. Store in an air-tight container until ready to use.

In a large bowl, toss together the mango, cucumber, carrot, capsicum, radish, watercress, coriander and basil.

Just before serving, heat up a fry pan with 2 tablespoons of olive oil, add the paprika and swirl the pan around to combine. Put in the prawns and toss to coat. This is a quick process, you merely want to coat the prawns with the hot paprika oil and not cook it any further. The small amount of heat will curl the prawns slightly.

Place the salad on a serving plate, top with the prawns, drizzle over the dressing and sprinkle with the dried shrimp "dukkah".

Notes: Shallow fry the dried prawns in oil a little at a time until crispy. Do not over crowd the pan. Drain the fried prawns on paper towels.

Garlic flakes are available from Asian grocery stores. To make your own, simply use a mandolin to shave thin garlic slices, dry them out on paper towels and fry them on low-medium heat until crispy and golden. Don't be tempted to increase the heat as the garlic will burn.

½ cup picked fresh coriander
  leaves, keep stems for dressing
½ cup picked fresh Thai basil
  leaves

DRESSING
Zest of 1 lime
4 tablespoons lime juice
4 teaspoons fish sauce
2 tablespoons sweet chilli sauce
  or 2 tablespoons raw sugar
2 teaspoons brown rice vinegar
2 teaspoons finely chopped garlic
2 teaspoon finely chopped
  coriander stems
2-3 hot Thai chillies, finely
  chopped

Laksa Prawn Bisque

SERVES 10-12

I made this with poached lobsters for a client's gala dinner and it was so well received. Soup plates were coming back to the kitchen empty and almost licked clean! This is a really beautiful bisque, with delicious flavours of a laksa broth enriched by pure prawn essence and subtle aromats. It's worth the effort.

6-8 large prawns, trimmed, left
  whole
16 cockles, soaked in water for
  30 minutes
30 pippies or clams, soaked in
  water for 30 minutes
Coconut cream
Micro coriander

PRAWN OIL
125 ml (½ cup) oil
2 cups fresh prawn heads and
  shells

SPICE PASTE
20 g large dried red chillies,
  deeded, soaked in hot water
10 g fresh turmeric

To make the prawn oil, heat about 125 ml (½ cup) oil in a medium-sized saucepan over medium heat. Add 2 cups of fresh prawn heads and shells and cook until the shells are golden and the oil is a deep pinkish amber. This will take anywhere from 30 minutes to 1 hour. Strain the oil into a glass jar, cover tightly and keep in the fridge.

For the spice paste, place the dried chillies, turmeric, garlic, onion, lemongrass, fresh chillies, coriander root, shrimp paste and candlenut in a food processor and blend until smooth.

Pour 7 tablespoons of oil into a medium-sized saucepan and place over medium heat. Add the spice paste and cook until fragrant. Remove and set aside in a bowl.

Use the same pan to make the bisque. Over medium heat,

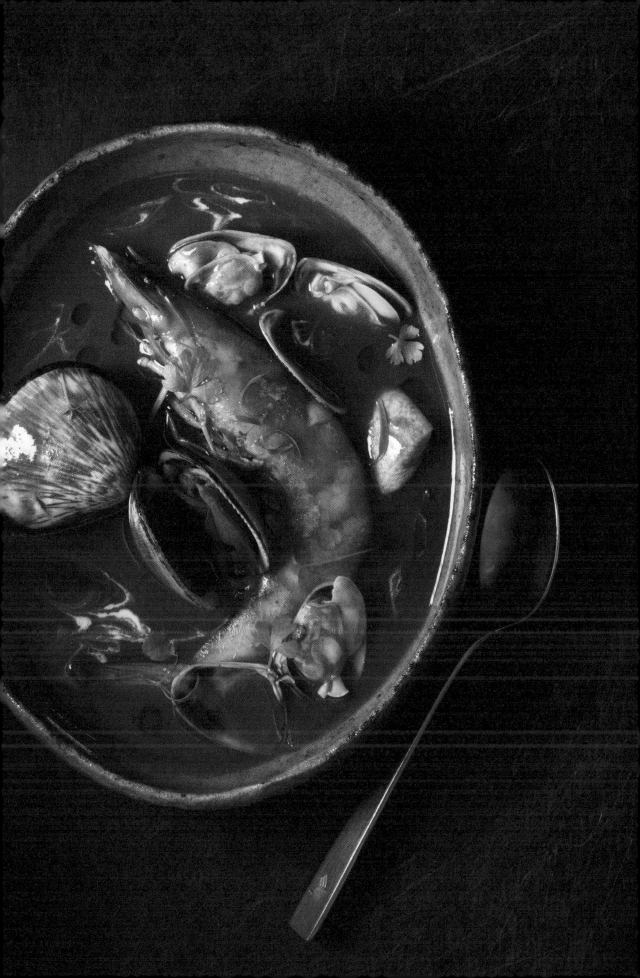

4-5 cloves garlic
130 g red Spanish onion
35 g lemongrass, white root-end
  only
15 g fresh large red chilli
10 g coriander roots
10 g belacan (shrimp paste),
  wrapped in foil, cook on a
  hot pan for 2-3 minutes on
  both sides
5 g candlenuts
7 tablespoons oil

PRAWN BISQUE
1.5 kg fresh prawn heads and
  shells (lobster, crayfish shells
  can also be included)
2.5 litres vegetable stock or
  water
30 g palm sugar
30 g salt
2 tablespoons oil

add 2 tablespoons of oil and fry the prawn head and shells until they turn pink and become very fragrant. Deglaze with ½ cup water, scrapping the bottom of the pan. Add the spice paste, salt and sugar, then the remaining stock or water. Lower the heat, cover and simmer for 30 minutes.

Remove from heat. Pour everything (including the shells and heads) into a blender. Ensure there is a gap for the hot air to escape, then blend until fine. Sieve the mixture, pressing down with a ladle to extract as much flavour as possible, then sieve again. Return the strained bisque to the saucepan, taste and adjust seasoning to your liking.

For the whole jumbo prawns, keep the shells intact but remove the intestinal tracts by piercing through the shells with a fork to gently pull the tract out.

Just before serving, bring a saucepan of water to the boil. Put in the prawns, turn off the heat and allow the prawns to poach for 2-3 minutes depending on their size. Poach the cockles and pippies along with the prawns and allow the residual heat to cook them. Remove as soon as the shells open. Set aside.

To serve, place a prawn and some shellfish in each bowl or soup plate and ladle on the bisque. Drizzle lightly with coconut cream, prawn oil and sprinkle over a little micro coriander.

Note: If you'd like to add poached lobster to the bisque, here's how you cook it. Place lobsters in the freezer for about an hour to put them to sleep. Fill a large pot with water and bring to the boil, submerge whole lobster and poach for about 5-7 minutes depending on the size. The internal temperature of the lobster should reach 60°C (140°F). Remove from the boiling water and dunk immediately into a basin of cold water to stop further cooking. When cool enough to handle, twist the head off, then use a pair of kitchen scissors to cut through the shell of the underbelly to the tail. Carefully remove all the meat. Slice into medallions to serve in the bisque. Remember to keep the shells to make the bisque.

Monk Fish Stir-Fried with Fermented Black Beans

SERVES 4

As monk fish is a fairly firm fish, it works well in a stir fry. If you can't find it at your local fishmonger, go for other similar textured fish, like ling.

500 g (1.1 lbs) monk fish or other firm white fish, sliced on the diagonal to 1-cm (0.4-in) pieces
1 heaped tablespoon cornflour for dusting
5 cloves garlic, peeled, finely julienned
25 g (0.9 oz) young ginger, peeled, finely julienned
2 tablespoons fermented dried black beans, rinsed
2 large stalks spring onions, cut into 6 cm lengths
½ teaspoon tapioca flour mixed with 2 tablespoons of water
2 large sprigs coriander, washed, root and stem finely chopped, leafy ends cut to 6-cm (2.4-in) lengths
1 teaspoon chilli flakes, or to taste
Oil

MARINADE
2 teaspoons soy sauce
2 teaspoons mirin
1 teaspoon sesame oil
1 teaspoon freshly cracked black pepper

SEASONING
2 teaspoons soy sauce
1 teaspoon mirin

Marinate the fish with the soy, mirin, sesame oil and black pepper. Set aside.

Mix the seasoning of soy and mirin. Set aside.

Heat a wok or fry pan with about 4 cm (1½ in) of oil over medium-high heat. Dust the fish in cornflour then fry until lightly golden. Drain on paper towels.

Remove all but about 3 tablespoons of oil in the wok. Increase the heat to high, toss in the garlic, ginger, fermented dried black beans and spring onions. Fry for a minute, then deglaze with the prepared soy and mirin seasoning.

Quickly add the tapioca flour slurry, stirring continuously for a few seconds. (If it thickens too much, add another tablespoon or two of water). Now add the fish and coriander and toss until just coated. Sprinkle with chilli flakes and serve immediately.

Note: If you do not wish to shallow fry the fish, then add the raw marinated fish after the garlic, ginger, fermented black beans and spring onions. Stir fry carefully so as not to break up the fish, then continue with the deglazing before adding the tapioca slurry and coriander. Don't forget to dust with the chilli flakes before serving.

Grilled Smoked Scarmoza and Stewed Apricots with Salsa Verde

SERVES 4 AS A STARTER OR SMALL PLATE

Scarmoza, a cheese from the mozzarella family, is known for its stretchy, curd-like consistency when melted. You can also use fior di latte, or fresh mozzarella. I prefer the smoked version of these cheeses.

This is a delicious starter or a light lunch when served with some extra-crunchy sourdough bread. I love scattering all the ingredients on a large board or platter for all to share. If you prefer individual servings, let your creativity take over. Note that this dish is best served with the cheese just warm.

250 g (8.8 oz) smoked scarmoza, fior di latte or smoked mozzarella, sliced thinly
1 Lebanese cucumber, shaved into ribbons
Black pepper, freshly cracked
1 heaped tablespoon micro herbs (micro cress and micro garnet)
Pinch of sumac
1 heaped tablespoon toasted almond slivers
Olive oil

STEWED APRICOTS
100 g (3.5 oz) dried apricot
2 tablespoons raw sugar
1 vanilla bean, halved, deseeded, pod retained
2 strips lemon peel
2 sprigs rosemary

SALSA VERDE
2 tablespoons freshly chopped coriander
1 green chilli, sliced thinly
2 teaspoons baby capers
Zest of 1 lemon
Squeeze of lemon juice
2-3 tablespoons olive oil
1-2 teaspoons champagne vinegar or apple cider vinegar
½ teaspoon raw sugar
Pinch of sea salt
Black pepper, freshly cracked

Start by making the stewed apricots. This is really an apricot compote and, essentially, we are going to cook the dried apricots until they soften. The cooking time will depend on the quality of your dried apricots.

Place the apricots, sugar, vanilla bean seeds and pod, lemon peel and rosemary sprigs along with 250 ml (1 cup) of water in a small saucepan. Cover, bring to the boil, lower flame to simmer for about 1-1½ hours until the apricots become soft and the liquid thickens to a syrup. If your apricots are exceptionally firm, add more water a little at time and cook until tender. Don't worry if they are of different textures. Once they soften, you can either leave them whole or mash them a little with a fork. However, don't mash them thoroughly – remember you are not making apricot jam but a compote, so you still want large chunks to be visible.

Make the coriander salsa verde by mixing all of its ingredients together.

Preheat your oven and the griller to 220°C (425°F). Place the slices of cheese on a baking sheet lined with greaseproof paper. Grill for 5-10 minutes until the cheese softens. If you have a blow torch and would like more charred bits, torch parts of the surface until it browns.

To serve, place the cheese slices organically on a platter or wooden board. Spoon over teaspoons of stewed apricots and coriander salsa, add the cucumber ribbons, then scatter over the micro herbs, cracked black pepper, sumac and toasted almonds. Drizzle over some olive oil and serve immediately.

Fried Cabbage with Mustard Seeds and Chilli

SERVES 4

Here is an incredibly quick to cook yet delicious traditional Indian vegetable dish.

4 cups shredded white cabbage
15 g (0.5 oz) young ginger,
  peeled, sliced then finely
  julienned
5 cloves garlic, peeled, thinly
  sliced, then julienned
2 large hot green or red chillies,
  thinly sliced on the diagonal
1 teaspoon black mustard seeds
Sea salt to taste
Oil

Heat 2–3 tablespoons of oil in a large fry pan over high heat. Add the ginger, garlic and chillies, and cook until lightly golden. Add the mustard seeds and allow to pop. Toss in the cabbage and cook until it is softened to your liking. Season with salt.

Kalette Fried with Bacon

SERVES 4

Kalettes are a hybrid of kale and Brussels sprouts. This is a simple and delicious dish that is great served either piping hot or at room temperature.

155 g (5.5 oz) kalette, large
  pieces halved lengthways
3 garlic cloves, crushed, skin
  removed and finely chopped
60 g (2 oz) bacon, cut into small
  batons
Pinch of chilli flakes or to taste
1 stalk spring onion, finely
  chopped
Pinch of sea salt or to taste
2 tablespoons olive oil

Bring a large pot of water to the boil. Prepare a large basin of ice-cold water on the side. Blanch the kalette briefly in the boiling water then immediately dunk them into the basin of cold water. Drain well.

In a large fry pan, heat up 2 tablespoons of olive oil over medium to high heat. Add the garlic and fry for 1–2 minutes. Put in the bacon and fry until caramelised and crispy. Toss in the blanched kalette and cook to your liking. I like my vegetables a little crunchy. If you prefer them more tender, cook for a little longer. Add the chilli flakes, spring onions and season with salt. Toss well. Serve.

Spiced Smoked Eggplant with Grated Coconut

SERVES 4

It was so difficult to create a pretty picture of this dish. To photograph it in the way it's cooked does it no justice. I was determined to find a way to photograph it because it is so delicious and worth your time and effort. The beauty of Indian spices enables a very simple dish to taste that good. Now that I've talked it up, I hope you enjoy it!

400 g (14 oz) eggplant
2½ tablespoons cold-pressed, extra-virgin coconut oil

1 small onion, peeled, halved, finely sliced
10 g (0.4 oz) ginger, peeled, coarsely grated
2 cloves garlic, peeled, coarsely grated
1 stalk curry leaf, stem discarded
1 large hot green chilli, finely sliced
25 g (¼ cup) fresh grated coconut
½ teaspoon ground cumin
½ teaspoon hot paprika
½ teaspoon ground turmeric
½ teaspoon sea salt
¼ cup roughly chopped coriander leaves and stems
Wedge of lime

Roast the eggplant over an open flame until completely charred. Place the charred eggplant in a glass bowl and cover tightly with cling film until cool enough to handle. Then remove and discard the charred skin, keeping the flesh whole. Set aside.

Place 2 tablespoons of coconut oil in a small-medium fry pan and heat over medium heat. Fry the onion, ginger, garlic, chilli, curry leaf until lightly charred and softened. Add the grated coconut and cook for a further few minutes. Add the cumin, paprika, turmeric, salt and the remaining half tablespoon of coconut oil. Toss well.

Pour this mixture into a food processor and blitz until well blended but not completely smooth. Pour into a bowl. You may also leave the coconut masala unblended.

Halve the flesh of the eggplant lengthways, then into quarters and then eighths taking care not to slice all the way through.

Slip the eggplant onto the same frypan, scatter over the masala, cover and cook over medium heat for a further 5 minutes. Remove from heat, scatter over the chopped coriander and serve immediately with a wedge of lime.

Notes: When removing the charred skin off the eggplant, as tempted as you might be, do not wash the eggplant. You will introduce unwanted moisture and dilute the flavours.

You may substitute fresh grated coconut with 25 g (¼ cup) of dried shredded coconut simmered in 60 ml (¼ cup) water until softened.

Roasted Cauliflower and Herbs with Spiced Oil and Yoghurt Dressing

SERVES 2-4

This is such a great way to cook cauliflower, spiced up and pan seared till golden, then smothered with yoghurt and topped with lots of fresh herbs.

2 steaks of cauliflower, 1.5-cm (0.6-in) thick
3 tablespoons olive oil
1 knob of butter
Sea salt to taste
1 teaspoon brown mustard seeds
2 sprigs curry leaves
1 teaspoon cumin seeds, toasted, roughly ground
1 teaspoon coriander seeds, toasted, roughly ground
½ teaspoon dried chilli flakes
½ teaspoon sweet paprika
1 teaspoon ground turmeric
1 tablespoon almond flakes, toasted
½ cup coriander leaves

YOGHURT DRESSING
2 heaped tablespoons Greek yoghurt
1 teaspoon honey
½ teaspoon ground cumin
½ Lebanese cucumber, shredded

Make the yoghurt dressing by combining all its ingredients. Set aside in the fridge.

Fill a large pot with water and bring to the boil. Blanch the cauliflower for 2 minutes, remove, place on a rack and let it dry.

Heat 1 tablespoon of olive oil and the butter in a large fry pan over medium-high heat. Sprinkle in a pinch of salt, then add the cauliflower steaks and any florets that have fallen off and cook for a couple of minutes on both sides until golden. Remove and drain on paper towels.

Put the remaining 2 tablespoons of olive oil into the same pan and fry the mustard seeds and curry leaves. Swirl the pan around to allow the seeds to pop. Add the cumin, coriander, chilli flakes, paprika, turmeric and a good pinch of salt. Toss well. Remove from heat.

Place the cauliflower steaks on a serving plate, drizzle with the spiced oil and all the spice bits from the pan, sprinkle over with almond flakes and fresh coriander and spoon on a dollop of the yoghurt dressing.

Stir-Fried Shredded Greens

SERVES 4

This will become your staple stir-fry vegetable dish. It's fairly substantial yet light and delicious.

5 cloves garlic, peeled, finely
   chopped
150 g (5.3 oz) carrots, peeled,
   thinly sliced on the diagonal,
   julienned
150 g (5.3 oz) white or savoy
   cabbage, shredded
150 g (5.3 oz) French beans,
   thinly sliced on the diagonal
150 g (5.3 oz) garlic scapes,
   garlic flowers or garlic shoots,
   sliced to 6-cm lengths
150 g (5.3 oz) five-spiced firm
   tofu, thinly sliced into strips
50 g (1.8 oz) tang hoon (bean
   thread vermicelli), softened in
   hot water, cut into 8-cm (3-in)
   lengths
2 tablespoons Shoaxing wine
2 tablespoons soy sauce
1 tablespoon oyster sauce
1 teaspoon sesame oil
White pepper
100 g (3.5 oz) bean sprouts, root
   tips removed
Oil

Heat 2 tablespoons of oil in a wok or a large saucepan over high heat. Fry the garlic for a minute, then add the carrots, cabbage and French beans. Cook for 3-4 minutes until slightly softened, stirring regularly. Put in 1-2 tablespoons of water if necessary to help steam the vegetables and avoid burning.

Toss in and combine the garlic scapes, tofu and vermicelli. Deglaze with Shoaxing wine, then add the soy sauce, oyster sauce, sesame oil and white pepper. Stir well.

Finally throw in the bean sprouts and immediately remove from the heat. The residual heat will be enough to remove the rawness of the sprouts yet keep them crunchy. Serve immediately.

Yam Cake

MAKES A 20 X 6 CM (7.8 X 2.4 IN) ROUND CAKE

This is a dish from my childhood! My mother used to make it quite frequently and it is still one which I absolutely love! I could never wait for it to cool because it's soft and delicious straight out of the steamer. When cold, slice into thin pieces and pan fry till crispy!

650 g (1.4 oz) yam (taro)
25 g (0.9 oz) dried shiitake
    mushrooms
45 g (1.6 oz) thinly sliced streaky
    bacon
40 g (1.4 oz) dried prawns,
    soaked briefly, roughly
    chopped
3 cloves garlic, skin discarded,
    finely chopped
½ teaspoon raw sugar
2 teaspoons freshly cracked white
    pepper
4 teaspoons fish sauce
1 teaspoon sea salt
120 g (4.2 oz) rice flour
125 ml (½ cup) oil
¼ cup crispy shallots

TOPPING
½ cup chopped chye poh
    (preserved radish), rinsed to
    remove excess salt, drained
Sugar to taste
2 large red chilies, finely diced
2 large stalks spring onions,
    finely sliced
Oil

Skin the yam and cut them into 1-cm (0.4-in) batons. This should yield 550 g (1.2 lbs) of prepared yam.

Soak the dried shiitake mushrooms in water to rehydrate. Add enough water to this mushroom liquid to make 750 ml (3 cups) and set aside. Thinly slice the mushrooms then roughly chop them up.

Bring a steamer filled with water to the boil. Rub 1 tablespoon of oil on the inside of a 20 x 7 cm (7.8 x 2.8 in) baking or steaming dish.

Heat 5 tablespoons of oil in a hot wok over medium heat. Add the bacon, dried prawns and garlic, and fry for 1 minute until lightly coloured. Add the mushrooms and fry for a couple of minutes. Then add half teaspoon of sugar and 2 teaspoons of white pepper. Stir to mix well.

Put in the yam and stir fry to combine. Then add the mushroom water, the fish sauce and ½ teaspoon salt. Stir well, then cover the wok and bring to the boil. Allow the yam to cook until tender, about 10-15 minutes. Then use your spatula to roughly chop the yam.

Mix the rice flour with 250 ml (1 cup) of water. Lower the flame and stir the rice flour slurry into the yam. Stir well until fully combined. If you think the mixture looks a little thick and pasty, add a little more water, a couple of tablespoons at a time (see note overleaf). Add the remaining oil and crispy shallots and mix well. Pour into the greased pan and level out with a spatula.

Steam on high heat for about 55-60 minutes.

To make the topping, heat 2 tablespoons of oil in a fry pan over medium heat. Toss in the preserved radish and fry for 2 minutes. Add a pinch of sugar. Remove from the heat then toss in the chillies. Allow to cool slightly, then mix in the spring onions. Scatter on the steamed yam cake.

Note: The amount of water you will need will largely depend on the quality of the yam. Yam with a high percentage of starch, which will feel slightly more powdery when you cut into it, will need a little more water. You are looking for a soft yet pasty consistency of mashed yam prior to steaming. However, if you prefer a softer yam cake, add an extra 3-4 tablespoons of water.

Bean Sprouts, Chilli and Herb Salad

SERVES 4

Both the Chinese and Koreans have a bean sprout salad. For both, I prefer to use Korean bean sprouts because of its chunkiness.

500 g (1.1 lbs) bean sprouts, tips of tails removed
2 large red chillies, finely sliced on the diagonal
1 cup loosely packed coriander leaves
1 cup loosely packed diagonally sliced spring onions
¼ cup crispy shallots

DRESSING
2 tablespoons soy sauce
1 tablespoon sesame oil
1 tablespoon chilli oil
2 cloves garlic, crushed, skin discarded and minced with a pinch of salt
1 teaspoon black sesame seeds, toasted
1 teaspoon white sesame seeds, toasted
½ teaspoon sugar
Freshly cracked black pepper
1 teaspoon Lao Gan Ma chilli sauce (optional)

Prepare a large basin of icy-cold water.

Bring a large pot of water with 1 heaped tablespoon of salt to the boil. Blanch the bean sprouts for 10 seconds. Drain and immediately dunk them into the cold water for a few minutes to cool. This stops the cooking process and keeps them crisp. Drain well.

Mix the soy sauce, sesame oil, chilli oil, minced garlic, sesame seeds, sugar, pepper and chilli sauce, if using.

Toss all the ingredients together, including the coriander leaves, spring onions and crispy shallots, and serve at room temperature

Buddha's Delight Salad

SERVES 4

The original version of this divine vegetarian dish, traditionally enjoyed by Buddhists, is served by custom in Chinese homes on the first day of the Lunar New Year. I've created a fresh salad version for what is normally stir fried or braised.

100 g (3.5 oz) fresh shiitake
  mushrooms, sliced to ½-cm
  (0.2-in) thickness
100 g (3.5 oz) fresh woodear
  fungus, torn into bite-size
  pieces
250 g (8.8 oz) small tofu puffs,
  cut into half on the diagonal
2 Lebanese or ½ a telegraph
  cucumber, halved, then sliced
  on the diagonal
4 red radish, sliced thinly on a
  mandolin
1 cup snow peas, stems and
  stringy bits removed, blanched
  for about 40 seconds in boiling
  water
2 large red chillies, sliced thinly
  on the diagonal
2 stalks spring onions, sliced
  thinly on the diagonal
1 cup fresh coriander leaves
2 teaspoons white sesame seeds,
  toasted
2 tablespoons crispy shallots

SESAME SOY DRESSING
8 teaspoons soy sauce
2 tablespoons brown rice vinegar
1 tablespoon sesame oil
8 teaspoons vegetable, rice bran
  or grapeseed oil
3 teaspoons raw sugar
2 teaspoons lemon juice
2 teaspoons finely-grated ginger

Make the dressing by placing all the ingredients in an empty jar. Tighten the lid and shake till well combined. I always make extra dressing to keep in the fridge. Simply double the recipe.

Place the mushrooms, tofu puffs, cucumber, radish, snow peas, chillies, spring onions, fresh coriander and sesame seeds in a large mixing bowl. Pour over the dressing and toss to combine. Top with crispy shallots. Serve immediately.

Spiced Quinoa, Cauliflower and Crushed Almonds

SERVES 4

The way to make vegetables beautiful and tasty is to cook them with delicious flavours. Cauliflower and spices are a match made in heaven.

85 g (3 oz) raw quinoa, rinsed and drained through a fine sieve

2 cups cauliflower florets

2 tablespoons cold-pressed, extra-virgin coconut oil

1 large Spanish red onion, peeled, halved, finely sliced

4 cloves garlic, peeled, coarsely grated

15 g (0.5 oz) young ginger, peeled, coarsely grated

2 long hot green chillies, sliced on the diagonal

2 stalks of curry leaves

1 teaspoon black mustard seeds

1 teaspoon cumin seeds, dry toasted and ground

1 teaspoon chilli powder (optional)

2 tablespoons curry powder

½ teaspoon sea salt, or to taste

½ teaspoon raw sugar, or to taste

2 large bunches coriander, leaves picked, stems and roots finely chopped

1 tablespoon crushed toasted almonds

Place the quinoa and 180 ml (¾ cup) water or stock in a small saucepan. Cover and bring to the boil. Lower the heat and cook until all the water has been absorbed and grains are cooked to al dente.

Heat the coconut oil in a large fry pan over high heat. Add the onions, garlic, ginger, chillies, and the coriander roots and stems. Cook for a couple of minutes, then push the ingredients to one side of the pan.

In the middle of the pan, add the curry leaves and mustard seeds along with another tablespoon of coconut oil. Stir until the mustard seeds start to pop. Add the cumin, chilli powder, curry powder, salt, sugar and cauliflower florets. Toss to coat.

Add a tablespoon or two of water, cover with a lid and cook for a few minutes until the cauliflower is tender but still has a crunch. Remove from heat. Toss in the cooked quinoa and adjust seasoning to your taste if required. Finally, add the coriander leaves, toss through and sprinkle over crushed, toasted almonds. Serve.

Falafel

SERVES 4-8

I love a good falafel, crunchy and green with lots of herbs and spices. The biggest tip in making falafel is to start with dried chickpeas. Soak them overnight. Canned chickpeas are a no-no. They are way too mushy, sloppy and does not produce an authentic dish!

FALAFEL
300 g (10.5 oz) dried chickpeas, soaked in water overnight, drained well
5 cloves garlic, peeled
1 medium Spanish onion, peeled, roughly chopped
½ cup chopped fresh coriander root, stem and leaves
¼ cup chopped parsley
2 teaspoons cumin seeds, toasted and ground
2 teaspoons coriander seeds, toasted and ground
3 green cardamom pods, crushed, shells discarded, seeds ground
2 teaspoons hot paprika
1½ teaspoon sea salt
½ teaspoon raw sugar

Oil for deep frying

DRESSING
280 g (1 cup) Greek yoghurt
½ teaspoon ground cumin
½ teaspoon honey

Place all the falafel ingredients in a food processor and blend until finely ground but not pasty. Rest for 30 minutes in the fridge.

Preheat at least 5-8 cm (2-3 in) of oil in a medium-sized saucepan or a wok. The temperature should be about 180°C (355°F). Take two tablespoons or an ice cream scoop of falafel mix and roll it into a ball with the palms of your hand. Repeat with the remaining mixture.

When the oil is hot, deep fry the falafels until golden brown. Drain well on some paper towels.

Combine the ingredients for the yoghurt dressing and serve it with the falafel.

Zucchini, Lentil and Herb Salad

SERVES 4

Zucchini isn't the most exciting vegetable in terms of flavour. However, slice it then char it and it becomes something quite special. Here's a recipe using the humble zucchini with puy lentils, lots of fresh herbs, chillies and molasses, molasses, molasses!

This salad is great on its own or served up with a couple of fried or poached eggs or some seared chicken tenderloins.

200 g (1 cup) puy lentils, rinsed well, strained
3 small zucchini, sliced lengthways, 3-mm (0.1-in) thick
1-2 large fresh red chillies, halved lengthways
Smoked salt
Cracked black pepper
Olive oil
½ cup chopped fresh coriander
½ cup chopped spring onions
Chilli flakes
¼ Tahitian lime or 2 calamansi limes
2 tablespoons grape molasses
2 tablespoons pomegranate molasses
¼ cup pine nuts, toasted
Crispy shallots

Put the lentils and 400 ml of water in a small saucepan. Bring to the boil and cook until al dente. Remove from the heat and drain well.

Place the zucchini strips and chillies in a large mixing bowl. Season well with smoked salt, black pepper and olive oil.

Preheat a large fry pan or griddle pan over high heat. Sear the strips of zucchini on both sides until nice and golden but still has a bite. Place in a large mixing bowl and set aside. Next, sear the chillies until blistered and lightly charred. Slice on the diagonal and add to the seared zucchini.

Add the lentils to the zucchini and chillies, along with the coriander and spring onions. Season well with a good pinch of smoked salt, cracked pepper and chilli flakes. Squeeze over the lime juice, add the grape and pomegranate molasses along with a good glug of olive oil. Toss well, top with the pine nuts and crispy shallots.

Spiced Buttered Couscous

SERVES 4

If you treat couscous purely like rice or grains, you'll realize that you can jazz it up with lots of flavours. This dish is buttery and fragrant with loads of Indian spices and fresh herbs. It can replace any spiced rice and is a great accompaniment to roast meats or fish.

300 g (1½ cups) couscous

3 tablespoons olive oil or cold-pressed, extra-virgin coconut oil

2 stalks curry leaves

2 medium onions, halved, peeled, thinly sliced

4 cloves garlic, thinly sliced

1 green chilli, thinly sliced

1½ teaspoons cumin seeds, toasted, coarsely ground

1 teaspoon coriander seeds, toasted and ground

3 green cardamom pods, toasted, crushed, seeds extracted and ground

½ teaspoon ground cinnamon

½ teaspoon garam masala

½ teaspoon hot paprika

500 ml (2 cups) chicken stock or vegetable stock, heated till hot

40 g (1.4 oz) butter

40 g (¼ cup) currants or chopped raisins

1 loosely packed cup roughly chopped mint, reserve some for topping

1 loosely packed cup roughly chopped parsley, reserve some for topping

1 loosely packed cup roughly chopped coriander, reserve some for topping

2 tablespoons pine nuts, toasted

2 tablespoons almond slivers or flakes, toasted

Heat the oil in a large saucepan or casserole dish over medium-high heat and fry the curry leaves until crisp, remove and set aside. In the same pan, add the onions and sauté until golden and lightly charred, about 5 minutes. Add the garlic and chilli and cook for 1 minute. Toss in the cumin, coriander, cardamom, cinnamon, garam masala and paprika and stir to combine. Remove from heat and set aside.

Place the couscous in a bowl, add the amount of hot stock according to the packet instructions, and cover tightly. Leave to steam for 10-15 minutes.

Remove the cover, add the butter, and fork through the couscous to loosen. Add the spiced onion mixture and mix well. Season to taste with salt, add currants or raisins, herbs, nuts, fried curry leaves and toss to combine. Top with reserved herbs.

Serve with the Indian Slow-Roasted Spiced Lamb (page 67).

Hearty Rice Bowl

SERVES 4

This dish is the epitome of clean food! It's easy to prepare and just relies on super-fresh ingredients. Feel free to substitute with other fresh vegetables that you love.

400 g (2 cups) cooked brown rice
1 ripe avocado, halved and sliced
1 medium cucumber, julienned
1 cup fresh snow peas, stems removed, finely sliced on the diagonal
2 nori sheets, finely sliced into strips
1 tablespoon sesame seeds, toasted
2 heaped tablespoons kimchi
2 stalks spring onions, finely sliced
4 eggs, soft boiled, sunny side up or poached

GINGER AND SOY VINAIGRETTE
2 tablespoons soy sauce
1½ scant tablespoons brown rice vinegar
3 teaspoons sesame oil
10 g (0.4 oz) young ginger, peeled, finely grated
2 teaspoons raw sugar
2 tablespoons oil

PICKLE
50 g shredded red cabbage
2 tablespoons white vinegar
2 tablespoons sugar
2 tablespoons water
Pinch of salt

Start by making the ginger and soy vinaigrette. Place all ingredients in a clean glass jar, screw the lid on and shake vigorously until well combined.

To make the pickle, mix the white vinegar, sugar, water and salt in a glass bowl. Stir until the sugar and salt dissolves. Toss in the shredded red cabbage and leave to pickle. You'll need to let it sit for at least 30 minute, tossing every 10 minutes or so. As soon as the cabbage has wilted but still crunchy, it's ready. This can be made days ahead and stored with the pickling liquid in a clean, airtight container in the fridge.

To serve, divide the rice into four serving bowls and spoon on all the various toppings, finishing with the toasted sesame seeds and a tablespoon or more of the dressing. Eat fresh!

Black Rice, Fruit, Nuts and Herb Salad with Orange and Pomegranate Molasses Vinaigratte

SERVES 4

I really love the nuttiness of black rice. It is sometimes known as Forbidden Black Rice, the name used by the Chinese since the 17th century. This was the rice specially kept for the emperors because it was believed that their nourishing qualities promoted good health and long life. These days, you can buy black rice from most supermarkets and health-food stores. I don't serve black rice as a staple but add it to salads such as this one.

185 g (1 cup) black rice
2 large, sweet, juicy oranges
1 large ripe avocado, diced
80 g (½ cup) pomegranate seeds
1 large red chilli, finely sliced
100 g (½ cup) white quinoa,
  cooked till al dente
125 g (1 cup) pecans, toasted
2 stalks spring onions, finely
  sliced
2 large sprigs fresh coriander,
  roots removed, stems and
  leaves roughly chopped
2 tablespoons flaked almonds,
  toasted

DRESSING
Orange juice squeezed from skin
2 tablespoons pomegranate
  molasses
2 tablespoons brown rice vinegar
  or apple cider vinegar
1 tablespoon honey
2-3 tablespoons grapeseed oil or
  light olive oil

Place the rice in a small saucepan, add 375 ml (1½ cups) of water, cover and bring to the boil. As soon as it boils, lower the heat, stir with a spoon, scraping the bottom of the saucepan. Cover and simmer until all the water has been absorbed. It's important not to cook the rice until it's soft and mushy; you want it al dente. Stir with a fork and allow to cool.

To prepare the oranges, cut off the top and bottom of each orange so they sit flat on a chopping board. Slice off the skin and pith of the oranges from top to bottom, then slice out the segments between the membranes. Set aside.

Squeeze into a bowl as much juice as possible from the remaining flesh left with the skin. Mix it with all the other ingredients for the dressing in a clean, glass jar.

Just before serving, mix all the salad ingredients, except for the avocado. Drizzle on the dressing and toss. Finally, add the avocado and gently toss. Serve immediately.

Note: I find that the best way to extract pomegranate seeds from a fresh pomegranate is to first halve the pomegranate across the middle. Then, holding half in your palm, cut side facing down, knock the fruit with a wooden spoon until all the pomegranate seeds have fallen out.

Black Rice Salad with Soy Vinaigrette

SERVES 4

Black rice in any salad makes it substantial, hence great for any light lunch. This recipe produces a nutty, wholesome and incredibly delicious dish!

185 g (1 cup) black rice, rinsed and drained

1 cup diced (150 g, 5.3 oz) fresh tofu or tau kwa (firm tofu)

½ cup edamame, blanched, drained

1½ cups small watercress sprigs

2 stalks spring onions, finely chopped

¼ cup mixed pepitas (pumpkin seeds) and sunflower seeds, toasted

¼ cup roasted, unsalted cashew nuts

½ cup mixed micro herbs (radish, watercress, coriander, celery)

1 heaped tablespoon crispy shallots

DRESSING

2 tablespoons soy sauce

2 tablespoons mirin

1 tablespoon brown rice vinegar

2 tablespoons oil

½ teaspoon raw sugar

1 heaped teaspoon finely grated ginger

Cut the tofu into 1-cm (0.4-in) cubes. Heat a small pan with 1 cm (0.4 in) oil and shallow fry the tofu until lightly golden. Set aside.

Place the rice in a small saucepan, add 375 ml (1½ cups) of water, cover and bring to the boil. As soon as it boils, stir with a spatula, scraping to loosen any bits at the bottom of the saucepan. Lower the heat right down, cover and simmer until all the water has been absorbed. If you like the grains a little softer, add another 1-1 ½ tablespoons of water at the start.

Fork through the rice and allow to cool. Then toss together with the edamame, watercress, spring onions, pumpkin seeds, sunflower seeds, cashew nuts and fried tofu. Pour over the dressing, toss to combine then spoon onto a serving plate. Top with the micro herbs and crispy shallots. Serve immediately.

Note: If you prefer more dressing, double the amounts for the dressing recipe.

Forbidden Black Rice and Herb Salad

SERVES 4

This is a beautiful black rice salad with lots of hearty fresh greens, seeds and nuts. It's so vibrant and looks amazing along with any spread you place on the table. It is also easy to make in large quantities. Just be sure to cook your rice to al dente and allow it to cool before tossing in the fresh herbs. You'll be sure to receive many exclamations of "oh wow" from your guests when they see this dish.

185 g (1 cup) black rice, rinsed and drained
1 medium carrot, peeled, finely julienned
1 Lebanese cucumber, finely julienned
½ cup spring onions, finely chopped
½ cup roughly chopped coriander leaves and stems
½ cup roughly chopped mint
½ cup roughly chopped curly parsley
½ cup roughly chopped Thai basil
1 large red chilli, finely sliced into rings
½ cup frozen edamame beans, blanched in boiling water for a minute or two
¼ cup shaved small red radish
¼ cup toasted peanuts, roughly chopped
Crispy shallots

DRESSING
4 tablespoons lime juice
1 tablespoon brown rice vinegar
4 tablespoons oil
1 tablespoon palm sugar or to taste
1 small red bird's eye chilli, finely chopped
1 clove garlic, peeled, finely chopped
1 tablespoon finely chopped coriander root and stem

Place the rice in a small saucepan, add 375 ml (1½ cups) of water, cover and bring to the boil. As soon as it comes to a boil, lower the heat right down and simmer until all the water has been absorbed. If you like the grains a little softer, add another 1–2 tablespoons of water at the start.

Fork the rice through and allow to cool. Then toss together with the salad ingredients except for the toasted peanuts and crispy shallots. Pour over the dressing, toss to combine then spoon onto a serving plate. Top with the toasted peanuts and loads of crispy shallots. Serve immediately.

Spiced Rice, Eggplant and Zucchini Masala in Filo Pastry

SERVES 4

This is a real festive dish totally inspired by pastilla, a Moroccan pie. It does take a little while to pull together but totally worth it when you present it at the dinner table!

EGGPLANT & ZUCCHINI MASALA
1 eggplant (500 g, 1.1 lb)
300 g (10.5 oz) zucchini, halved lengthways, sliced on the diagonal
2 tablespoons cold-pressed extra-virgin coconut oil
1 large (250 g, 8.8 oz) onion, peeled, halved, thinly sliced
2 stalks curry leaves
1 heaped tablespoon grated ginger
1 heaped tablespoon grated garlic
2 tablespoons finely chopped coriander stem and root
2 large hot green chillies, sliced thinly
2 teaspoons curry powder
1 teaspoon ground cumin
1 teaspoon ground coriander
1 teaspoon cinnamon
1 teaspoon hot paprika
1 teaspoon turmeric
1½ teaspoons sugar
1½-2 teaspoons salt or to taste
125 ml (½ cup) water
Zest and juice of ¼ lime
1 cup fresh coriander leaves, roughly chopped

SPICED RICE
1 tablespoon cold-pressed extra-virgin coconut oil
3 cloves garlic, peeled, coarsely grated
2 stalks curry leaves
4 cardamom pods, crushed lightly
1 large cinnamon stick

To prepare the eggplant for the masala, place the eggplant over the open flame of a stove top or barbecue and cook until the skin is charred all over and the flesh has softened. Set aside to cool slightly. Carefully remove all the charred skin and the stem. Do not rinse! Pull the flesh apart into strips and set aside.

To prepare the spiced rice, place the saucepan over medium heat. Heat the coconut oil, add the garlic, curry leaves, cardamom, cinnamon, cloves, star anise, and dried chillies, and fry for 2 minutes until fragrant. Add the coriander, cumin, and turmeric then stir in the rice. Put in the lentils, stock, salt and pepper. Stir well and bring to the boil. Lower the heat to a simmer, cover and allow the rice to cook. It won't take long, 5-10 minutes at most. As soon as the rice is cooked, remove from heat and stir through with a fork. Toss in the currants, nuts and fried onions. Season with more salt if needed. Set aside to cool.

To prepare the masala, heat the coconut oil in a medium-sized pan over medium-high heat. Add the onions and cook for 10-15 minutes until softened and charred around the edges. Add the curry leaves and allow to pop for about 10 seconds. Then add the ginger, garlic, chopped coriander root and stems and chillies. Cook until fragrant, about 2-3 minutes. Add the curry powder, cumin, coriander, cinnamon, paprika, turmeric and stir well. Then toss in the sliced zucchini and charred eggplant strips. Season with sugar and salt and add the water. Cook until the vegetables have softened and the dish is saucy and thick. Add the lime zest and juice, along with the coriander leaves and stir well. Taste and adjust the seasoning with extra salt if required. Set aside to cool.

Preheat your oven to 190°C (375°F).

Just before compiling, mix the 1½ cups chopped coriander leaves into the rice.

4 cloves

1 star anise

2 small dried chillies

2 teaspoons ground coriander

2 teaspoons ground cumin

½ teaspoon ground turmeric

250 g (1½ cups) basmati rice, washed and drained

150 g (¾ cups) green or puy lentils, cooked in boiling water until al dente (about 30-40 minutes), drained

330 ml (1⅓ cups) vegetable stock

1 teaspoon sea salt

Freshly ground black pepper

80 g (½ cup) dried currants

70 g (½ cup) toasted pine nuts or slivered almonds

2 large (500 g, 1.1 lbs) onions, peeled, halved, thinly sliced and separated, shallow fried in oil until golden, drain well

1½ cups fresh coriander leaves, roughly chopped

PASTRY

6 sheets filo pastry

50g butter, melted

YOGHURT DRESSING

420 g (1½ cups) Greek yoghurt

2 teaspoons honey

Pinch of salt

Zest of 1 lemon

1 teaspoon cumin seeds, toasted, coarsely ground

1 Lebanese cucumber, coarsely grated or julienned

1 tablespoon oil

½ teaspoon chilli powder or paprika

FINAL TOUCH

1 tablespoon icing sugar, sifted

1 teaspoon ground cinnamon

Line a 30-cm (12-in) dish or fry pan with filo by first buttering the base and sides of with a pastry brush. Place one sheet of filo pastry to cover about three-quarters of the base and let the excess hang over the sides. Overlap this with a second filo sheet so that it hangs over the opposite side of the dish. Butter the filo slightly, including the sides, then lay on two more sheets of pastry using the same method. Butter the base slightly, then place one sheet in the middle of the base.

Divide the rice into two lots, fill the base with one lot, top with the eggplant and zucchini masala then cover with the remaining rice. Cover the rice with the last sheet of filo. Butter the pastry lightly, then gently bring all the overhanging bits to the top, scrunching it gently and making sure that the rice is covered. Lightly butter the top once more and bake for 1 hour until golden. If the top is not golden enough, increase the temperature to 200°C (395°F) in the last 5 minutes of cooking.

To make the yoghurt dressing, mix together the yoghurt, honey, salt, zest, cumin and cucumber. Heat the oil, sprinkle over the chilli powder or paprika and drizzle this mixture over the yoghurt.

Just before serving, mix the icing sugar and cinnamon and dust generously over the filo pastry. Offer the yoghurt dressing on the side. This dish is great eaten hot or at room temperature.

Fried Tofu with Dried Shrimps and Curry Leaves

SERVES 4-6

I've been growing a curry leaf plant on my balcony in Sydney for several years. The little cutting given to me by my friend Jo has grown and provided a continuous supply of curry leaves. In addition to the fact that curry leaves have an abundance of health benefits, they are a lovely addition to dishes.

With the addition of the curry leaves, this dish has an eclectic mix of ingredients, somewhat like the brilliant mix of cultures in my hometown, Singapore.

400 g (14 oz) tau kwa (firm tofu) or fresh tofu, whole or cut into 4x4x2-cm (1.5x 1.5x0.8-in) pieces, patted dry
2 tablespoons rice flour
½ teaspoon coarsely ground Szechuan pepper
Pinch of sea salt
Oil
Kecap manis (Indonesian sweet soy sauce)
1 heaped tablespoon chopped spring onions
1 heaped tablespoon fresh coriander
1 tablespoon dried shrimp 'dukkah' (pages 96 and 98)

TOPPING
6 cloves garlic, finely chopped
1 large hot red chilli, finely diced
1 large hot green chilli, finely diced
20 g (0.7 oz) dried prawns, soaked in water for 30 minutes, then pounded coarsely in a mortar and pestle
2-3 stalks curry leaves
Pinch of sea salt
Pinch of raw sugar
Oil

Mix the rice flour, Szechuan pepper and salt in a small bowl.

To prepare the topping, heat 4 tablespoons of oil in a small to medium sized fry pan over low to medium heat. Fry the garlic and chillies for a couple of minutes until the colour just starts to turn a little golden, then add the dried prawns and cook for a further minute. Toss in the curry leaves, salt and sugar,and stir to combine. Remove from heat and pour into a clean bowl.

Cover the surface of a non-stick fry pan with oil and place over medium heat. Dust the tofu in the rice-flour mix and pan fry the tofu until golden on all sides. Place on a serving dish, drizzle over some kecap manis. Add toppings, then sprinkle over the spring onions, coriander and dried shrimp "dukkah". Serve immediately.

Note: Do not use silken tofu for this dish as it is too soft.

Audra's Tauhu Goreng

Crispy Tofu with Peanut Sauce

SERVES 4-6

A good peanut sauce is an incredibly versatile condiment. Forget the gluggy ones with peanut butter added to it. An authentic peanut sauce, which is also eaten with satay, is made with ground peanuts and definitely worth the effort.

Peanut sauce can be frozen for a few months if it is vacuum sealed or stored in an airtight container. I often freeze them in serving-sized portions so that it is easier to thaw and use.

400 g (14 oz) fresh tofu or tau kwa (firm tofu), patted dry, cut into 6-8 pieces
2 tablespoons rice flour
¼ teaspoon sea salt
¼ teaspoon pepper
Oil

PEANUT SAUCE
20 g (0.7 oz) galangal, finely chopped
30 g (1 oz) long, dried, red chillies, soaked in hot water to soften, drained, roughly chopped
6 cloves garlic, crushed, skin discarded
10 g (0.4 oz) belacan (shrimp paste)
2 stalks lemongrass, white root-ends, bruised
1 tablespoon (25 g) tamarind paste, soaked in 140 ml (³/₅ cup) water until softened, sieved to produce about 130 ml (½ cup) tamarind puree
400 g (14 oz) raw peanuts, unsalted, roasted, ground till coarse
5 tablespoons raw sugar
1-1½ teaspoons sea salt
100 ml (²/₅ cup) oil

TOPPING
1 medium cucumber, peeled
Crispy shallots
Red sliced chilli
Micro coriander (optional)

Place the galangal, dried chillies, garlic and belacan in a food processor and blend to form a fine paste.

Heat 100 ml (²/₅ cup) of oil in a large saucepan over medium heat. Add the paste along with the lemongrass and cook until fragrant, about 5-8 minutes. Scrape in all the tamarind puree and stir for a couple of minutes. Then add the peanuts along with about 600 ml (2½ cups) of water. Stir well to combine.

Bring the sauce up to the boil, then add the sugar and salt. Drop the heat to medium, cover and cook for a further 10-15 minutes stirring constantly until it starts to thicken slightly. Be careful as it will spit. If it starts to spit too much, reduce the heat to low. You may have to cook for a little longer until the sauce thickens. Taste and adjust sweetness and saltiness to your preference. If you prefer a thinner sauce, add a further 100 ml (²/₅ cup) of water at this stage and adjust the seasoning with more salt and sugar according to taste.

Cut the cucumber into ribbons with a peeler.

Fill a fry pan with 2.5 cm (1 in) of oil. Heat over medium-high heat to about 180°C (355°F). Season the rice flour with salt and pepper and toss the tofu lightly in it. Deep or shallow fry until the tofu is lightly golden. Drain.

Place on the serving plate, scoop over the peanut sauce, top with cucumber ribbons, crispy shallots, sliced chillies, and micro coriander, if using. Serve immediately.

Note: For a less-spicy sauce, discard the seeds of the dried chillies before soaking them. You can also fry the tofu without dusting with flour.

Audra's Yellow Dal

SERVES 4

I cook dal a lot at home. It's one of the greatest Indian vegetarian dishes ever created that is incredibly nutritious and can feed masses very cheaply. Yellow split peas are known to have one of the highest percentage of dietary fibre and a rich source of complex carbohydrates. The kids love it and usually ask that I serve it with appam (page 138), one of their favoured dishes. You can replace yellow split peas with green split peas or combine them. My recipe packs in lots of spices and flavours, the way we like it.

300 g (1½ cups) dried yellow split pea, rinse and soaked for 2-3 hours, drained
Pinch of asafoetida (optional)
Cold-pressed, extra-virgin coconut oil
1 medium onion, peeled, halved, thinly sliced
1 teaspoon cumin seeds
1 teaspoon black mustard seeds
2 sprigs fresh curry leaves
3 cloves garlic, peeled, coarsely grated
20 g (0.7 oz) ginger, peeled, coarsely grated
3 small dried hot red chillies
2 large red hot chillies, finely sliced
2 heaped tablespoons finely chopped coriander leaves, stems and roots
1 heaped teaspoon curry powder
1½ teaspoons sea salt or to taste

In a medium-sized saucepan over medium-high, cook the soaked yellow split peas in 1 litre (4 cups) of water and the asafoetida, if using, until tender. This should take about 30 minutes. Set aside.

Heat 2 tablespoons of coconut oil in another medium saucepan over high heat. Add the onions and cook until lightly golden with slightly charred bits. Push the onions to one side of the pan. Add the cumin and mustards seeds to other side and temper until the mustards seeds start to pop. You many need to lower the heat to prevent the spices from burning. Add the curry leaves and stir until slightly blistered. Then include the garlic, ginger, both types of chillies, coriander stems and roots, tossing for another minute or so or until the chillies blister slightly. Add the curry powder, mix well and cook for another minute until all the ingredients have caramelised.

Feel free to add another tablespoon of coconut oil into the masala mixture at this stage if the mixture dries up. Next, pour the dal into the saucepan of masala and mix well scraping the bottom of the pan. Season with salt, simmer for 5 minutes, and remove from heat. Serve.

Like all curries, dals are best cooked ahead of time to allow the flavours to develop.

Note: Asoefatida can be found at all Indian grocery stores.

Dal and Kale

SERVES 4

I often create dishes based on what I find in the fridge. We eat a lot of kale and there's usually a big bunch in the chiller, and we also always have dal stocked up in the pantry. So, this dish was waiting to be created! One of the great things about dal is its versatility. I love the combination of the earthy, rich, green leaves of kale with dal. This dish is beautiful over brown rice.

300 g (1½ cups) dried yellow or green split peas

140 g (5 oz) kale leaves, roughly chopped

Cold-pressed extra-virgin coconut oil

1 medium onion, peeled, halved, thinly sliced

1 teaspoon cumin seeds

½ teaspoon black mustard seeds

2 sprigs curry leaves

3 cloves garlic, peeled, thinly sliced, finely julienned

20 g (0.7 oz) ginger, peeled, thinly sliced, finely julienned

3 green chillies, finely chopped

2 small dried red chillies

1 small bunch coriander, leaves picked, stems and root finely chopped

½ teaspoon ground cumin

1 teaspoon ground coriander

1 heaped teaspoon curry powder

1½ teaspoons sea salt or to taste

Soak the split peas in water for at least 4 hours or overnight, then drain.

In a medium-sized saucepan over medium-high heat, cook the soaked split peas in 1 litre (4 cups) of water until tender but not mushy. This should take about 30 minutes. Set aside.

Heat 2 tablespoons of coconut oil in another medium-sized saucepan over high heat. Add the onions and cook until lightly golden with slightly charred bits. Push the onions to one side of the pan. Put the cumin and mustards seeds on the other side and temper until the mustard seeds start to pop. Lower the heat if the pan gets too hot as you don't want to burn the spices. Add the curry leaves and stir until slightly blistered. Then add the garlic, ginger, both types of chillies, coriander stems and roots and toss for another minute or until the chillies blister slightly. Add the curry powder, ground cumin and coriander, mix well and cook for another minute until all the ingredients have caramelised.

Toss in the kale and cook until slightly wilted. At this stage, feel free to add another tablespoon of coconut oil into the masala mixture if the mixture dries up. Next, pour the dal into the saucepan of masala and stir well, scraping the bottom of the pan. Season with salt, simmer for 5 minutes until the kale is wilted completely. Remove from heat and serve.

Like all curries, dal dishes like this one are best cooked ahead of time to allow the flavours to develop.

Sticky Gula Melaka Tempeh with Kaffir Lime

SERVES 4

I never liked tempeh as a child. My mother would cook a sambal goreng with tempeh, prawns, tofu and long beans and I'd always eat the prawns, tofu and long beans and leave the rest. Give me a plate of these sticky tempeh anytime now, and there will be nothing left on the plate.

250 g (10.5 oz) tempeh 3 cloves garlic, crushed, skin
   discarded
5 g (0.2 oz) galangal, roughly
   chopped
1 stalk lemongrass, white root-end, finely chopped
5 g (0.2 oz) belacan (shrimp paste), wrapped in foil and toasted on a dry pan
1 Spanish red onion, peeled, halved lengthways, finely sliced
2 large red chillies, finely sliced on the diagonal
1 tablespoon tamarind pulp, soaked in 4 tablespoons water, rendered and sieved
1 tablespoon shaved gula Melaka
2 tablespoons kecap manis (Indonesian sweet soy sauce)
6 kaffir lime leaves, thinly sliced
Oil

Slice the fresh tempeh into 3-mm (0.1-in) thick pieces, and 2-mm (0.08-in) for frozen tempeh.

In a wok or saucepan with 2.5 cm (1 in) of oil, fry the tempeh till golden. Remove and drain on some paper towels.

Pound or blend the garlic, galangal, lemongrass and shrimp paste to a fine paste.

Heat 2 tablespoons of oil in a wok or fry pan over medium-high heat. Add the spice paste and cook until fragrant and dry. Push the paste to one side of the pan, add a tablespoon more of oil to the pan and fry the onions and chillies until slightly charred.

Stir in the tamarind puree, shaved gula Melaka and kecap manis. Toss in the fried tempeh and combine until well coated and sticky. Sprinkle over the kaffir lime leaves and serve.

Note: You may use both fresh and frozen tempeh for this recipe. However note that fresh tempeh tends to be more crumbly then frozen ones. So don't be alarmed if they fall apart during cooking. They also tend to crisp up more easily and stay crispy for longer. If you're using frozen tempeh, to achieve a similar result, thaw, then slice them a little thinner, about 2-mm thick.

Appam

Indian Pancakes

MAKES 12-14

It's a coincidence that Appam, which is one of my favourite dishes is, according to my father, a dish which my grandmother, who passed away before I was born, used to make all the time.

This quick method uses yeast in the recipe. Without the addition of yeast, the batter must be allowed to ferment for 24-48 hours depending on the temperature. When the weather is warmer, you will find that the batter ferments very quickly. So a few hours of rising might just be sufficient. You want a consistency that is slightly thicker than pouring cream. If the batter thickens too much, add a little water and mix well.

200 g (7 oz) raw basmati rice, soaked in water for 4 hours, drained
50 g (1.8 oz) cooked basmati rice
60 ml (¼ cup) coconut water
315 ml coconut milk
1½ teaspoons sugar
1 teaspoon sea salt
¼ teaspoon dry, active yeast
Oil

Blend the raw rice, cooked rice and coconut water until smooth. Then add the coconut milk, sugar, salt and yeast and continue blending until smooth. Set aside at room temperature for a few hours or overnight to ferment. If the weather is warm, the batter might only take 2-3 hours to double in size when fermented.

Wipe the surface of an appam wok, known as an appachatti, with a piece of paper towel dipped in oil, then place over medium heat. Pour in a ladle of batter, then lift the wok and twirl the batter around in a clockwise motion so that the batter lines about three-quarters up the sides of the wok. Place the lid on and cook for a few minutes until the pancake is fully cooked, with the edges lacy and crisp. The appam should come off the pan easily.

Repeat with the remainder of the batter.

Serve with my yellow split pea dal (page 134) or orange sugar available in Indian grocery stores.

Note: The traditional, round-bottomed, cast iron appam pan I use cooks one pancake at a time. It measures 21cm (8.25 in) in diameter and 6 cm (2.4 in) in height. I was given a non-stick one which measures 17 cm (6.6 in) in diameter and 7 cm (2.75 in) in height. They are both easily available in Indian cookware shops.

Indian-Style Scrambled Eggs

SERVES 4

This simple dish was totally inspired by a radio listener who won tickets to a dinner I hosted in Singapore. It is ingenious, wickedly delicious and showcases everything I love about culinary cultural influences!

8 eggs
Freshly ground black pepper
Sea salt to taste
2 large green chillies, finely sliced
1 medium onion, peeled, halved, finely sliced
2 cloves garlic, peeled, finely sliced
10 g (0.4 oz) young ginger, peeled, finely julienned
1 cup finely chopped fresh coriander stems and leaves plus 1 tablespoon extra
1 teaspoon garam masala
¾ teaspoon ground cumin
¾ teaspoon ground coriander
¾ teaspoon chilli powder
Olive oil

Whisk together the eggs, pepper and salt in a bowl.

In a medium-sized, non-stick fry pan, heat about 3-4 tablespoons of oil over medium heat. Fry the chillies, onion, garlic and ginger for 2–3 minutes until lightly charred. Add the cup of chopped coriander, along with the garam masala, cumin, coriander and chilli powder. Season with salt.

Pour in the eggs. Allow to set slightly, about 10 seconds, then using a spatula, stir the eggs, moving them around the pan until they are almost cooked. I find it easiest to use a flexible-edge silicon spatula.

Remove from heat and portion over slices of toasted sourdough bread. Top with the extra fresh coriander and grated parmesan cheese. Serve immediately.

Grilled Halloumi, Avocado and Fried Egg Salad with Lemon Honey Dressing

SERVES 4

Sometimes, the simplest recipes are the most satisfying. This dish is not just a great start to your day but works for lunch and dinner as well. It's full of freshness and quite substantial.

180 g (6.3 oz) halloumi, sliced into 3-mm (0.1-in) thickness
1- 2 avocados, quartered
4 eggs, fried or poached
200 g (7 oz) mixed cherry and yellow grape or baby heirloom tomatoes, some halved, some left whole
1½-2 cups wild baby rocket or frisée (curly endive)
40 g (¼ cup) edamame, blanched till al dente
1 cup roughly chopped fresh coriander
Salt
Zest of a lemon
Juice of ½ lemon
Freshly cracked black pepper
Pinch of sumac
Olive oil

VINAIGRETTE
1 teaspoon honey
Freshly cracked black pepper
1 bird's eye chilli, finely chopped (seeds optional)
Juice of ½ lemon
3½ tablespoons extra-virgin olive oil

Put all the ingredients for the vinaigrette into a glass jar, cover with the lid and shake until well combined.

Toss the tomatoes, rocket, edamame and coriander in a mixing bowl with a pinch of salt and a squeeze of lemon juice. Portion on serving plates.

Quarter the avocados and squeeze a little lemon juice over them to prevent discolouring. Add the avocados to each plate.

Cook the eggs as you wish, fried or poached. A good tip when frying eggs is to add a teaspoon of water in the hot pan after cracking in the eggs. Cover the pan to steam the top of the eggs for a minute. Place an egg on every serving plate.

Lastly, fry the halloumi in a non-stick pan placed over medium-high heat with a little olive oil until nicely golden on both sides. Transfer directly to the serving plates.

Season each plate with vinaigrette, lemon zest, black pepper, sumac, then a drizzle of olive oil. Serve immediately.

Ricotta Parcels

MAKES 20-24

Pastizzi is a very popular Maltese pastry with either ricotta or mushy peas inside. I love their puff pastry. The layers of crispy and delicious pastry is just incredible. This is a simplified version using regular puff pastry but it is just as good. Keep the parcels frozen and bung them in the oven for a quick bake when your craving hits.

4 sheets square puff pastry
1 egg, lightly beaten for egg wash
Nigella seeds

FILLING
600 g (1.3 lbs) fresh, full-cream ricotta
1 egg, lightly beaten
4 cloves garlic, peeled, finely grated
1 cup finely chopped spring onions
½ cup finely chopped fresh coriander
½ teaspoon freshly ground white pepper
½ teaspoon freshly ground black pepper
½ teaspoon ground coriander
1 heaped teaspoon lemon zest
Good pinch of sea salt
30 g (1 oz) pecorino cheese, finely grated

Preheat your oven to 200°C (395°F). Line two large baking sheets with silicon or grease-proof paper.

To make the filling, place the ricotta, egg, garlic, spring onions, fresh coriander, white and black pepper, ground coriander, lemon zest, salt and pecorino cheese into a large bowl. Stir and mix well to combine.

Run a knife down the middle of a sheet of puff pastry to create two rectangles. Work with a rectangular sheet of pastry at a time. Dollop a tablespoon of filling in the middle of the top, centre and bottom parts of the pastry leaving a gap between each. Fold one long side of the pastry over the filling and then fold the other side so that it overlaps the first fold in the middle. They don't need to overlap by a lot. It's also fine to leave the fold in the middle loose as this will encourage the pastry to gape open during baking to allow steam to escape.

Using a sharp knife, slice straight across or at a diagonal to create three parcels. Seal the open sides well either by pinching with your fingers or pressing with a fork. Place on the baking sheet. Repeat with the remaining pastry.

Brush with egg wash and sprinkle over the nigella seeds. Bake for about 25 minutes or until the pastry is golden and cooked through.

Szechuan-Style Sesame Soba with Poached Chicken

SERVES 4

This is, hands down, one of the dishes I love. Don't let its simplicity fool you. The combination of the black vinegar with tahini, soy and chilli oil does wonders. The fresh herbs and cucumber just lightens the mix. I'd be happy to eat this every day of the week and often I leave out the poached chicken to just keep it purely vegetarian. This dish is best served at room temperature.

240-300 g (8.5-10.5 oz) soba noodles
2 large stalks spring onions, finely chopped
1 medium bunch fresh coriander, roughly chopped
2 Lebanese cucumbers, sliced on the diagonal and julienned
120 g (4.2 oz) fresh tofu or tau kwa, cut into ¾-cm (0.3-in) cubes and lightly deep-fried
Crispy shallots

POACHED CHICKEN
300 g (10.5 oz) chicken breast
2 cloves garlic, crushed, skin discarded
1 large or 2 small stalks spring onion, chopped to 4-cm (1.5-in) lengths
3 slices ginger

DRESSING
2 tablespoons tahini
2 tablespoons Lao Gan Ma chilli sauce
4 tablespoons soy sauce
2 tablespoons black vinegar
1 tablespoon raw sugar
2 tablespoons water or chicken or vegetable stock
2 tablespoons chilli oil

To poach the chicken breast, place the garlic, spring onion and ginger in a small saucepan of water and bring to the boil. Gently lower the chicken breast into the water, ensuring it is fully submerged, and bring it back to the boil. Then immediately turn off the heat, cover and allow to sit until it cools. The residual heat will continue to cook the chicken. Remove the chicken and shred into long, thin strips with your fingers.

To make the dressing, mix all its ingredients together until well combined.

Cook the soba until al dente. Rinse under cold water to remove excess starch. Drain well. Toss in the dressing and spring onions, topped with coriander, cucumber, tofu, shredded chicken and crispy shallots. Serve immediately.

Note: I use made-in-China Lao Gan Ma brand chilli sauce for this dish. It's full of crispy onions, chillies and Szechuan peppers. For alternatives, look for chilli sauces that are cooked with dried crispy chilllies.

Sweet Potato Noodle Bowl

SERVES 4

This is my take on the Korean Bibim Naengmyeon. I bought a bowl of these noodles at a very small family-run takeaway kiosk at the Busan train station when Mom and I visited Korea a couple of years ago. We were headed to Seoul.

Once the train took off, I tucked into my noodles which came sealed along with a tiny, almost toy-like, 3-cm long plastic knife to slice open the wrapper. I thought the whole experience was just amazing, the attention to detail and the convenience factor, not to mention that the family members at the kiosk were such lovely people. Then I tucked into the noodles and immediately regretted that I didn't buy two bowls. All I could do was slowly slurp and enjoy the incredible noodles.

150 g (5.3 oz) Korean sweet-potato vermicelli noodles

1 tablespoon sesame oil plus extra

1 Lebanese cucumber or ½ telegraph cucumber, julienned

¼ cup mung bean shoots (optional)

1 cup bean sprouts, tailed

100 g (3.5 oz) fresh tofu or tau kwa (firm tofu) or tau pok (fried tofu puffs), cut into 1-cm (0.4 in) cubes

1 medium carrot, peeled, finely julienned

2 cups baby spinach or regular spinach leaves and stems, blanched, drained well

1 nashi pear, peeled, julienned, soaked in water with a little sugar added to avoid oxidizing

2 eggs, lightly whisked

2 stalks spring onion, finely chopped

2 toasted nori sheets, sliced into fine strips

1½ tablespoons white sesame seeds, toasted

SAUCE

2 cloves garlic, peeled, minced

5 g (0.2 oz) knob young ginger, peeled, finely grated

2 stalks spring onion, washed, cut into 4-cm (1.5 in) lengths

¼ nashi pear, peeled, roughly chopped

1 tablespoon gochugaru (Korean hot red pepper flakes)

2 tablespoons gochujang (Korean hot pepper paste)

1 tablespoon soy sauce

1 teaspoon brown rice vinegar or apple cider vinegar

1 tablespoon rice syrup

1 teaspoon sesame oil

1 teaspoon raw sugar

Salt

To make the sauce, blend all its ingredients together in a food processor along with 2 tablespoons of water until smooth. Set aside.

Bring a large pot of water to the boil. Cook the noodles according to instructions on the packet until al dente. Rinse thoroughly to remove excess starch. Drain well. When cool, toss with 1 tablespoon of sesame oil.

Prepare all your vegetables as required.

In a flat non-stick fry pan, cook the eggs into super-thin crepes. Roll them up together and finely slice.

If the noodles clump together, rinse through with warm water and drain very well. Toss the noodles with one teaspoon of sesame oil and 1–2 tablespoons of sauce. Then divide the noodles into serving bowls or place them on one large plate. Top with all the various toppings, finishing with the toasted sesame seeds and the remaining sauce. Serve at room temperature. Simply mix the ingredients with the sauce, then slurp.

This dish is very versatile, so feel free to replace with other vegetables. Grilled meats can also be added. My Grilled Gochujang Pork (page 58) works well with this dish.

Cold Soba with Shredded Greens, Nori and Ginger-Soy Dressing

SERVES 4-6

This is one of the ways I love to eat soba noodles. It's a take on zaru soba, the Japanese cold soba noodles served with a dipping sauce (tsuyu). It's fresh, light and just delicious! Feel free to use other vegetables.

240 g (8.5 oz) dried soba noodles

100 g (3.5 oz) snow peas, stem and stringy bit removed, finely sliced on the diagonal

150 g (5.3 oz) finely shredded savoy cabbage

4 stalks spring onions, finely chopped

1 teaspoon shichimi togarashi (Japanese pepper)

½ telegraph cucumber, sliced on the diagonal, julienned

2 toasted nori sheets, cut into strips

1 tablespoon sesame seeds, toasted

DRESSING

4 tablespoons soy sauce

4 tablespoons mirin

2 tablespoons brown rice vinegar

2 teaspoons sesame oil

1 heaped teaspoon finely grated ginger

Bring a medium saucepan of water to the boil. Cook the soba noodles until al dente. The time will depend on the brand you use. Check the cooking instructions and drop a minute or two of the total suggested cooking time. It's important not to overcook your noodles or the dish will be gluggy. In fact, it's better to undercook it slightly, like the true Italian way, with a bite in the middle. Drain and immediately dunk in cold water to stop the cooking and remove the excess starch. Drain well and set aside.

Mix all the ingredients for the dressing in a small glass jar.

Nori sheets are sold in a standard size everywhere. The best way to get even strips is to first cut it into half, then into quarters, then into eights. Now cut the small rectangles into strips along the shorter ends.

Just before you are ready to serve, toss together the noodles, snow peas, cabbage, spring onions, shichimi togarashi and the dressing according to taste (you may not need all of it). Place on a plate, then top with shredded cucumber, nori strips and toasted sesame. Serve immediately.

Home-Style Hokkien Mee Goreng

Hokkien Fried Noodles

SERVES 4

This is a reinvention of my mother's recipe. Super delicious! If you're using Hokkien noodles that are thick and yellow, you don't need to blanch them at all.

500 g (1.1 lbs) fresh Hokkien
  noodles, removed from packet
  and separated with a pair of
  chopsticks
200 g (7 oz) shelled medium
  prawns
8 cloves garlic, crushed, skin
  discarded, roughly chopped
6 large red chillies, roughly
  chopped
3 tablespoons dried prawns,
  soaked for 10 minutes
200 g (7 oz) fresh tofu or
  tau kwa (firm tofu), sliced into
  0.5x3-cm (0.2x1.2-in) pieces
1 medium Spanish red onion,
  peeled, halved, thinly sliced
2 slim and tender or 1 large leek,
  sliced on the diagonal into
  1-cm (0.4-in) slices
1 bunch choy sum or English
  spinach, cut into 6-cm (2.4-in)
  lengths
100 g (3.5 oz) fish cake, thinly
  sliced
½ teaspoon sugar
1 tablespoon soy sauce
2 tablespoons kecap manis
  (Indonesian sweet soy sauce)
Oil
200 g (7 oz) bean sprouts,
  tails removed
1 bunch Thai basil leaves, to give
1 cup
Juice of half a lime (optional)

Pound the garlic, chillies and dried prawns until a rough paste is obtained. Set aside.

Heat a wok or large non-stick fry pan over medium heat. Add 2 tablespoons of oil. Pan fry the tofu until lightly golden. Remove and set aside.

Add a further 4 tablespoons of oil into the wok. Over medium heat, add the pounded chillies, garlic and dried prawns and cook for 2-3 minutes until fragrant. Add the sliced onion and leek and cook for 2 minutes. Season with sugar.

Add the prawns and lightly sear them. Toss in the choy sum and fish cakes and cook for a further 2 minutes then add the noodles. Season with the sugar, soy sauce and kecap manis and add 2-3 tablespoons of water. Put in the tofu and bean sprouts and toss well.

Remove from heat and sprinkle in the basil leaves. Squeeze over the lime juice (if using) and serve immediately.

Szechuan Beef Noodle Soup

SERVES 4

This spicy soup has all the richness of a beef broth heavily spiked with lip-numbing Szechuan peppercorns and dried red chillies. It's addictive!

1 kg (2.2 lbs) gravy beef, shin beef or chuck steak, cut into 4-cm (1.5-in) cubes
2 tablespoons Szechuan peppercorns, toasted
1 teaspoon black peppercorns, toasted
4 star anise
4 cloves
¼ cup oil
15 cloves garlic, crushed, skin discarded
20 g (0.7 oz) ginger, sliced
2 onions (400 g, 14 oz), peeled, halved, then each into 6-8 wedges
4 large stalks spring onions, cut to 6-cm (2.4-in) lengths
1 cinnamon stick
10 large dried red chillies
4 dried Indian bay leaves
2 dried tangerine peels
2 ripe tomatoes, blanched, skin removed, roughly chopped
2 heaped tablespoons chilli bean paste
4 tablespoons Shaoxing wine
5 tablespoons soy sauce
2 litres (8 cups) water
15 g (0.5 oz) rock sugar or raw sugar

500 g (1.1 lbs) Shanghai noodles
500 g (1.1 lbs) baby bok choy
1 tablespoon crispy shallots
2 tablespoons chopped fresh coriander

Place the beef in a large pot, cover with boiling water and bring back to the boil. Boil for 5 minutes, then strain to remove the scum and set aside.

Tie the Szechuan peppercorns, black peppercorns, star anise and cloves in a muslin cloth.

In a 3-litre (100-fl oz) capacity, deep saucepan, add the oil and heat over high heat. Fry the garlic, ginger, onions and spring onions for about 3 minutes until lightly blistered. Add the muslin bag of spices along with the cinnamon, dried chillies, bay leaves and tangerine peel. Fry for a couple of minutes. Then stir in the tomatoes, chilli bean paste and deglaze with the Shaoxing wine followed by the soy sauce.

Include the beef in the saucepan and top with 2 litres (8 cups) of water. Bring to the boil and lower the heat to simmer. Cook covered for 1½-2 hours or until the beef is very tender and gelatinous. Season with sugar.

To serve, blanch the bok choy and drain them. Cook the noodles until al dente, drain well and place in serving dishes along with the vegetables. Top with the beef and soup. Scatter over some crispy shallots and chopped coriander.

Black Bean XO Sauce

MAKES 1¼ CUPS

This is a rich, indulgent and truly delicious condiment that can be used for just about everything. Try a spoonful or two over stir-fried French beans or a simple omelette with steamed Jasmine rice.

1 tablespoon dried, fermented black beans
20 g (0.7 oz) dried scallops, soaked in warm water till softened, shredded finely with your fingers
20 g (0.7 oz) dried prawns, soaked in warm water till softened
30 g (1 oz) smoked ham or lap cheong (Chinese sausage), finely diced
125 ml (½ cup) oil
20 g (0.7 oz) garlic, finely chopped
20 g (0.7 oz) ginger, finely chopped
100 g (3.5 oz) fresh, long, red and hot chilli, finely diced
5-10 g (0.2-0.2 oz) bird's eye chilli, finely diced
1 teaspoon sea salt
1 teaspoon raw sugar
2 heaped tablespoons finely chopped spring onions

Heat the oil in a medium-sized saucepan over medium heat. Fry the garlic, ginger and both chillies for 3-4 minutes until fragrant and slightly golden. Add the scallops and dried prawns and cook for 3-4 minutes until golden.

Lower the heat, stir in the ham or lap cheong and cook for 6-8 minutes until lightly golden. If you are using lap cheong, be careful as it will burn relatively easily due to its high fat content.

Add the fermented black beans and cook for about 1 minute. Season with salt and sugar. Fill a sterilised jar, cool, then store in the fridge.

Just before serving, warm through and fold in the chopped spring onions.

Note: You can make a straight-forward XO sauce by omitting the black beans.

Cumin Yoghurt Dressing

420 g (½ cup) Greek yoghurt
2 teaspoons honey
Zest of 1 lemon
1 teaspoon cumin seeds, toasted, coarsely ground
Pinch of salt
1 tablespoon oil
½ teaspoon chilli powder or paprika

Mix the yoghurt, honey, lemon zest, ground cumin, and salt.

Heat the oil and sprinkle over the chilli powder or paprika.

Drizzle this flavoured oil over the yoghurt mixture.

Pickled Vegetables

MAKES A LITRE JAR

I always have a jar of these lovely and very versatile pickled vegetables – a combination of carrots, cabbage, red chillies and little red radishes – sitting in my fridge. Feel free to change the vegetables you'd like to pickle. Just note that vegetables like purple cabbage will colour the pickling liquid and turn all your other vegetables purple!

This pickle keeps for quite a long time in the fridge, just be mindful of using a clean spoon when scooping them out. I find a pair of chopsticks does the job best.

2 leaves white cabbage, cut into bite-sized pieces
1 medium carrot, sliced into bite-sized pieces on the diagonal
1 small daikon, sliced into bite-sized pieces on the diagonal
2 red chillies, sliced into bite-sized pieces on the diagonal

PICKLING SYRUP
125 ml (½ cup) white vinegar
125 g (4.4 oz) sugar
125 ml (½ cup) water
3 whole cloves
Pinch of salt

To prepare the pickling syrup, place the vinegar, sugar, water, cloves and salt in a saucepan and bring to the boil. Remove and set aside to cool.

Ensure all the prepared vegetables are washed and dried well. Place in a sterilised glass jar and pour over the pickling syrup. You want to make sure the vegetables are submerged in the liquid. Note that as they pickle, they will soften slightly, allowing you to press them down into the liquid. Allow to infuse for at least 24 hours before serving. Store in the refrigerator.

Note: Avoid using metal or stainless-steel jars or containers as they tend to react with the vinegar and result in rather unpleasant tasting pickles. Adjust the amount of pickling liquid according to the amount of vegetables you intend to pickle and the jar you are using.

Variation: Add a tablespoon of soy sauce to the pickling liquid to give the pickle a touch of umami.

Chilli Miso Honey

MAKES ABOUT 100 ML, ABOUT HALF CUP

This sauce is great as a dipping sauce but also works well as a marinade for meats.

30 g (1 oz) miso
30 g (1 oz) gochujang (Korean hot pepper paste)
1 tablespoon honey
1 tablespoon mirin

Stir all ingredients together until well combined. Store in an airtight container in the fridge. It will last for months.

Haybee Hiam

Chillied Dried Prawn Floss

SERVES 4

This condiment deserves a special spot in your fridge. As long as I can remember, my mother always had a healthy supply of haybee hiam in her fridge. It's incredibly versatile and goes with everything, including plain steamed rice. A tablespoon added to fried bee hoon (rice noodles), fried rice or stir fried vegetables just takes the dish up a notch. As a kid I used to sprinkle it generously on buttered fresh bread and sandwich it with thin slices of cucumber. Bliss!

I like my haybee hiam relatively chunky so I blend all the ingredients coarsely.

200 g (7 oz) dried prawns, soaked in water for at least 2 hours, drained

1 medium (125 g, 4.4 oz) Spanish red onion or red shallots, peeled, roughly chopped

30 g (1 oz) garlic, crushed, skin discarded

30 g (1 oz) large red dried chillies, soaked in hot water for 2 hours, drained, roughly chopped

30 g (1 oz) large red fresh chillies, roughly chopped

1½ tablespoons raw sugar

½ tablespoon tamarind pulp, soaked in 3⅓ tablespoons of water, then sieved to obtain 1½ tablespoons tamarind puree

Good pinch of sea salt

2 tablespoons finely chopped kaffir lime leaves (optional)

½ cup oil (rice bran, vegetable)

Place the dried prawns in the food processor and pulse until coarsely ground. Make sure it's not too fine. Remove and set aside.

Coarsely blend the onion and garlic separately. Remove and set aside.

Finally, blend the dried and fresh chillies coarsely too.

Heat the oil in a large wok or fry pan over medium heat. Add the onion, garlic and chilli, stirring continuously for about 6 minutes until fragrant and a good amount of moisture has evaporated.

Toss in the dried prawns and cook for 5 minutes until really fragrant. Add the sugar, tamarind puree and a good pinch of salt and continue cooking for another 20-25 minutes or until the mixture is dry and crumbly. Make sure to stir frequently to avoid the bottom from burning. Adjust seasoning according to taste. If you decide to add the kaffir lime leaves, put them in in the last 5 minutes of cooking.

Serving ideas: Add a tablespoon of haybee hiam to stir-fry French beans with kecap manis, or to shredded cabbage with a dash of fish sauce, or to sliced ladies fingers (okra) and a pinch of salt.

Birthday Trifle

SERVES 10-12

A crowd pleaser but more importantly, my husband's favourite 'birthday cake'! A few bits to prep but all worth it in the end!

5 punnets assortment of
  strawberries, cherries,
  blueberries, and raspberries

VANILLA CHIFFON CAKE
140 g (5 oz) plain flour, sifted
1½ teaspoons baking powder
4 egg yolks
80 ml (1/3 cup) oil
125 ml (½ cup) water
150 g (¾ cup) caster sugar
2 teaspoons vanilla extract
5 egg whites
¼ teaspoon cream of tartar

JELLY
6 gold-strength gelatine leaves
375 ml (1½ cups) unsweetened
  cranberry juice
2 tablespoons caster sugar

VANILLA CUSTARD
400 ml (1.7 cups) full-cream
  milk
1 vanilla bean, seeds scraped
80 g (1.9 oz) caster sugar
30 g (1 oz) cornflour
4 egg yolks
100 ml (²/₅ cup) thickened
  cream

RUM CREAM
200 ml (⁴/₅ cup) thickened cream
1 tablespoon icing sugar, sifted
2 teaspoons rum

VANILLA CHIFFON CAKE
Preheat your oven to 180°C (355°F). Set aside a 20-cm (8-in) tall or 23-cm (9-in) regular chiffon cake tin.

Sift the flour and baking powder together in a mixing bowl. In a separate bowl, whisk together the egg yolks, oil, water, half the sugar and vanilla extract. Add the flour and whisk until smooth.

In an electric mixer with a whisk attachment, beat the egg whites and cream of tartar on medium-high speed until foamy. Increase to high speed. While the mixer is whisking, slowly pour in the remaining sugar and whisk until you get thick and glossy meringue.

Add a third of the meringue to the egg and flour batter and whisk until well combined. With confidence, gently fold in the remainder of the meringue until just combined. Be careful not to over mix or you will lose all the precious aeration.

Pour into the baking tin and bake for 45-50 minutes until cooked through. Remove from the oven and invert immediately to cool. Allow to cool completely before removing the cake from the tin.

JELLY
Soak the gelatine leaves in cold water to soften. Warm the cranberry juice and sugar over medium heat in a saucepan until the sugar dissolves. Squeeze out as much liquid as possible from the gelatine leaves and add to the cranberry mixture. Stir until it dissolves. Pour into a rectangular container and refrigerate until the jelly sets.

CUSTARD
Place the milk and vanilla seeds in a small saucepan and bring to the boil. Immediately remove from the heat and set aside.

In a separate mixing bowl, whisk together the sugar,

cornflour and egg yolks until pale and creamy. Gradually whisk in all the hot milk. Return the mixture back into the saucepan and stir over medium heat until the mixture thickens and the rawness of the cornflour disappears. Remove from the heat and pour into a glass bowl, place cling film directly on top of the custard and refrigerate to cool.

Once the mixture is cool and set, stir it up with a wooden spoon until smooth. In a separate bowl, whisk the thickened cream until soft peaks. Fold the cream into the custard starting with a couple of tablespoons to loosen the mixture, followed by the remainder. Refrigerate until ready to use.

RUM CREAM
Whisk the cream, icing sugar and rum together until soft peaks. Refrigerate until ready to use.

ASSEMBLY
When you are ready to assemble, let your creative juices flow. Just remember to create separate layers of fruit, cake, custard, jelly and cream and avoid the layers morphing together! Leave enough fruit for the final topping. Allow your finished creation to sit in the fridge for 20–30 minutes before serving.

Dark Chocolate Brownies
with Pecans and Rum-Soaked Prunes

MAKES 12-16

Decadent, indulgent, dark and delicious! These brownies are all about the chocolate so make sure you use good quality dark chocolate and cocoa powder. I love the addition of the prunes as it totally cuts through the richness.

100 g (3.5 oz) dried prunes, roughly chopped, soaked overnight in 3⅓ tablespoons rum
200 g (7 oz) 70% cocoa dark chocolate
180 g (6.3 oz) unsalted butter
110 g (3.8 oz) plain flour
¼ teaspoon baking powder
¼ teaspoon salt
15 g (0.5 oz) Dutch cocoa powder
220 g (1 cup) soft brown sugar
1 teaspoon vanilla extract
4 large eggs
50 g (½ cup) pecans, toasted, roughly chopped

Prepare the prunes a day or two ahead of baking. Soak them in the rum in a ceramic or glass dish and wrap it with cling film. Leave at room temperature overnight.

Preheat your oven to 170°C (338°F). Lightly grease and line a 20-cm (7.8-in) square tin with greaseproof paper.

Place the chocolate and butter in a mixing bowl over a saucepan of simmering water. Leave until almost melted, then remove from the heat and stir until smooth. Set aside to cool.

In a separate bowl, sift together the flour, baking powder, salt and cocoa powder.

Add the sugar to the cooled chocolate and butter mixture and whisk until combined. Add the vanilla extract, then whisk in the eggs one by one making sure the mixture is well combined after each addition. Fold in the dry ingredients, followed by the pecans and prunes until just combined.

Pour into the prepared tin and bake for 20 minutes.

Remove from the oven and cool in the tin before turning out to slice.

Note: For a non-alcoholic version, soak the prunes in strong, brewed English Breakfast tea.

Coconut Pandan Crepes with Gula Melaka and Coconut Pandan Cream

MAKES 12-16

This is my take on kueh dadar, delicious fragrant crepes filled with gula-Melaka-flavoured grated coconut. It's a wonderful way of turning a traditional Malay and Nonya snack into a modern dessert.

PANDAN JUICE
6 large pandan leaves
4 tablespoons water

BATTER
120 g (4.2 oz) plain flour
¼ teaspoon salt
1 egg, lightly beaten
200 ml (4/5 cup) coconut cream
100 ml (2/5 cup) coconut water
4 tablespoons pandan juice

FILLING
100 g (1 cup) freshly grated coconut (keep 15 g for the topping)
80 g (2.8 oz) gula Melaka, shaved
1 pandan leaf, torn into strips and knotted
3⅓ tablespoons water
Pinch of salt

COCONUT PANDAN CREAM
400 ml (1.7 cups) coconut milk
4 pandan leaves, torn into strips and knotted
80 g (⅓ cup) caster sugar
30 g (1 oz) cornflour
4 egg yolks
100 ml (²/₅ cup) thickened cream

GULA MELAKA SYRUP
50 g (1.8 oz) gula Melaka, shaved
1⅓ tablespoons water

PANDAN JUICE

Place the pandan leaves and water in a blender and blitz for a minute. Alternatively finely chop and macerate in a mortar and pestle. Strain through a fine sieve or cheese cloth pressing out as much juice as possible (about 3 tablespoons). Set aside.

BATTER

Sift the flour and salt into a medium-sized mixing bowl. Make a well in the center and pour in the beaten egg. While stirring with a wooden spoon, slowly add the coconut cream, coconut water and pandan juice. We want a thick and smooth batter, not one that is aerated. Set aside.

FILLING

Place the gula Melaka in a saucepan along with the pandan leaf and water. Cook over medium heat until the gula Melaka has dissolved. Pass through a sieve and return to the saucepan. Stir in all but 15 g of the grated coconut and salt, cook for a few minutes until well coated and dry. Set aside to cool. (If you are using dried shredded coconut, place 85 g of coconut along with 1 cup (250 ml) of water in a saucepan and cook until the liquid has almost evaporated.) Now add the sieved gula Melaka and salt to the coconut in a saucepan. Cook until well coated and dry.

CREPES

Lightly oil a non-stick fry pan and place over low heat. The size of the fry pan will determine the diameter of your crepe. I use a 20-cm (7.8-in) pan to make small ones. Pour about 2 tablespoons of the batter in the center and swirl the pan to coat the entire surface. You are looking to create a thin crepe. Adjust the flame between low and medium heat to cook the crepes.

When the crepe is cooked with a slight gold tinge at the base, transfer it onto a serving plate. You only need to cook one side of the crepe. Allow to cool. Cover with cling film. Repeat until all the batter has been used up. Separate each crepe with some cling film.

PANDAN COCONUT CREAM
In a small saucepan, bring the coconut milk and pandan leaves to a boil, then immediately remove from the heat and set aside.

Whisk together the sugar, cornflour and egg yolks in a large mixing bowl until pale and creamy. Gradually whisk in all the hot coconut milk. Return the mixture to the saucepan and whisk over medium heat until the mixture thickens. Remove from the heat, pour into a glass bowl, place cling film directly on top of the mixture and refrigerate to cool and firm up.

Once the mixture is cool, stir it up with a wooden spoon until smooth. In a separate bowl, whisk the thickened cream until soft peaks. Fold the cream into the custard starting with a couple of tablespoons to loosen the mixture, followed by the rest. Refrigerate until ready to use.

GULA MELAKA SYRUP
To make the syrup, place the gula Melaka and water in a small saucepan and bring to the boil. Once the gula Melaka has dissolved, pass through a sieve and pour back into the saucepan. Reduce the heat and cook until slightly thickened and syrupy. Remove and set aside to cool. Note that the syrup will thicken further when cool.

ASSEMBLY
To serve, dollop 1 tablespoon of the pandan cream on one corner of a crepe, then 1 heaped teaspoon of coconut filling over the cream. Fold the crepe into half, then again into quarters. Repeat with remaining crepes.

Serve crepes topped with the reserved freshly grated coconut, Coconut Pandan Ice Cream (page 168) and gula Melaka syrup.

Coconut Pandan Ice Cream

MAKES JUST UNDER A 1-LITRE (2-PINT) TUB

There are so many Asian desserts that are made with coconut and pandan. Here is a recipe with these classic ingredients in an ice cream! It's so simple, works so well, and one that's hard to resist. This ice cream goes well with my Coconut Pandan Crepes with Gula Melaka and Coconut Pandan Cream (page 164).

300 ml (1¼ cups) coconut cream
200 ml (4/5 cup) coconut water
4 pandan leaves, torn into
    strips and knotted
120 g (4.2 oz) honey
4 egg yolks

Prepare a large basin of ice water.

Place the coconut cream, coconut water and knotted pandan leaves in a saucepan, bring to the boil and remove from the heat immediately.

While the coconut mixture is on the stove, whisk the honey and egg yolks together in a mixing bowl until light and pale. Slowly whisk in the hot coconut milk mixture through a sieve. Return the mixture to the saucepan, cook on low-medium heat, stirring with a wooden spoon until the mixture coats the back of the spoon. A good way to test this is to run your finger over the spoon. The line should remain intact. Be careful not to overcook this or the custard will curdle. The temperature of the liquid should reach around 85°C (185°F).

Pour the custard mixture through a sieve into a mixing bowl sitting in a large basin of iced water and whisk until the mixture is cold.

Empty into a prepared ice cream maker and churn until the ice cream is smooth and creamy.

Transfer into a container, cover and freeze.

Cardamom and Honey Ice Cream

MAKES JUST UNDER A 1-LITRE (2-PINT) TUB

I love making ice cream with honey. It tends to have a much more mellow flavour and the sweetness doesn't take over. This ice cream has a lovely a hint of cardamom and is great on its own or sandwiched between my Cranberry and Pistachio Cookies (page 186).

250 ml (1 cup) milk
250 ml (1 cup) thickened cream
1 vanilla bean
8 green cardamom pods, cracked
⅛ teaspoon ground cardamom
120 g (4.2 oz) honey
4 egg yolks

Prepare a large basin with ice and a little water.

Place the milk, thickened cream, vanilla bean (pod and seeds) and both crushed and ground cardamom in a saucepan, bring to the boil then remove from the heat.

While the mixture is on the stove, whisk the honey and egg yolks together in a mixing bowl until light and pale. Slowly whisk in the hot milk and cream mixture through a sieve. Return the mixture to the saucepan, cook on low-medium heat, stirring with a wooden spoon until the mixture coats the back of the wooden spoon. A good way to test this is to run your finger over the spoon. The line should remain intact. Be careful not to overcook this or the custard will curdle. The temperature of the liquid should reach around 85°C (185°F).

Pour the custard through a sieve into a mixing bowl sitting in the large basin of iced water. Continue whisking until the mixture is cold.

Empty into a prepared ice cream maker and churn until the ice cream is smooth and creamy.

Transfer to a container, cover and freeze.

Fig, Rosemary & Vanilla Tarte Tatin with Vino Cotto

SERVES 8

If you are a fig lover like me, I don't think you'll need any convincing to give this recipe a go. It's a beautiful, luscious and decadent tart that will impress any guest you have. Make sure you pick good-quality ripe figs.

12 ripe black figs, halved
   lengthways
50 g (1.8 oz) caster sugar
50 g (1.8 oz) honey
2 tablespoons vinocotto
75 g (2.6 oz) unsalted butter
1 vanilla bean, halved, seeds
   scraped
1 stalk fresh rosemary
4 strips lemon peel
Juice of ¼ lemon
Pinch of salt
250 g (8.8 oz) puff pastry
Almond slivers, toasted
   (optional)

Preheat your oven to 200°C (395°F).

Place the caster sugar, honey and vinocotto in a 23-cm (9-in) fry pan that can be placed in the oven and heat over medium heat until the sugar and honey mixture starts to melt and caramelise. Allow the sugar mixture to turn an auburn colour, then whisk in the butter along with the vanilla bean pod and seeds, rosemary, lemon juice, and strips of lemon peel.

Sprinkle in a pinch of salt and allow the caramel to bubble away for a minute. Reduce the heat, stir in the lemon juice, then gently place the figs cut side down in a circular design all around the pan. Don't be afraid to squeeze the figs together. Cook for 2–3 minutes until the figs soften slightly and start to caramelize. Remove from the heat.

Roll out the puff pastry into about a ¾-cm (0.3-in) thick disc some 2 cm (0.8 in) wider than the pan. Place the pastry over the entire surface, tucking the edges down the side of the pan and bake for 25–30 minutes or until the pastry is cooked through and super golden.

Remove from the oven and rest for 5 minutes. Now place a large serving plate over the fry pan, hold onto the plate with one hand and flip the fry pan to turn it over.

Sprinkle over the toasted slivers of almonds and serve immediately with vanilla bean ice cream.

Note: Vino cotto is a syrup made from the must of freshly pressed premium dark grapes cooked down and cellared for months or years to give it it's unique flavour. You can purchase it from most specialty food shops. If you can't find it, feel free to use tawny port, muscat or balsamic glaze instead.

Fig, Almond & Honey Cake

SERVES 12-16

One of the many things I crave is to have a fig tree in my garden. One that bears lots and lots of fruit. You'd likely find me climbing it to reach that perfectly ripe fruit at the top. It's one of life's pleasures to be able to pick a ripe fruit, tear it apart and just enjoy it. Then, to be able to cook with it, put it into tarts, cakes, salads, roasts… the list is endless. For this recipe, make sure you pick up lovely ripe and juicy figs!

100 g (3.5 oz) fig jam (optional)
5-6 fresh large ripe figs (about 300 g, 10.5 oz), quartered
2 teaspoons honey
15 g (0.5 oz) almond flakes, toasted
180 g (6.3 oz) unsalted butter, at room temperature
150 g (¾ cup) caster sugar
3 eggs, lightly beaten
2 teaspoons vanilla extract or 1 plump vanilla bean, seeds scraped
180 g (6.3 oz) almond meal
80 g (2.8 oz) plain flour, sifted
Pinch of salt
80 g (2.8 oz) natural or Greek yoghurt

Preheat your oven to 190°C (375°F). Butter and line a 23-cm (9-in) loose-base or spring-form cake tin with greaseproof paper.

Cream the butter and sugar until light and fluffy. Slowly drizzle in the eggs while whisking, ensuring each addition is fully combined before the next little drizzle. Add the vanilla and whisk lightly. Fold in the almond meal, flour and salt until just combined. Then lightly fold in the yoghurt.

Roughly spread half the cake mix on the base of the tin. Spoon in the fig jam, if using. Spoon over the remainder of the mixture. Use a knife to make swirls in the cake mix then press in each fig flesh side up randomly over the top. Drizzle with honey and sprinkle over the almond flakes.

Lower the oven temperature to 170°C (338°F) and bake for about 60 minutes or until a skewer pierced into the middle of the cake comes out clean. Remove from the oven, cool the cake in the tin for about 10 minutes. Then remove and allow to cool completely on a cake rack.

Transfer the cake fig side up onto a cake stand. Sieve over some icing sugar and serve.

Note: If you are including the fig jam, choose one that is less sweet and has chunky bits of fig.

Macadamia, Apricot & Thyme Tart

SERVES 10-12

This combination of macadamia nuts, apricot jam and thyme makes the perfect frangipane tart. Slather on as much or as little apricot jam as you wish!

PASTRY
170 g (6 oz) plain flour, sifted
Pinch of salt
100 g (3.5 oz) cold unsalted
  butter, cubed
1 egg yolk
1 tablespoon cold water★

FILLING
100 g (3.5 oz) unsalted butter,
  slightly softened at room
  temperature
100 g (½ cup) caster sugar
2 eggs
2 teaspoons vanilla extract
100 g (3.5 oz) almond meal
1 teaspoon flour, sifted
40 whole macadamias

3 tablespoons apricot jam diluted
  with 1½ tablespoons water
Fresh thyme leaves

★ The amount of cold water needed for the dough will depend on the weather. In warm humid climates, you will not need as much water. Just add enough for the dough to come together.

Butter and lightly dust with flour a 24-cm (9.5-in) diameter loose-based tart tin.

To make the pastry, place the flour and salt in a food processor and blitz for 20 seconds until well combined. Add the butter and pulse until the mixture resembles breadcrumbs. With the motor running, add the egg yolk and cold water for the dough to come together. Empty onto a clean surface, gently pat together to form a flat disc, wrap with cling film and refrigerate for 20-30 minutes.

Preheat your oven to 180°C (355°F).

Roll the pastry out between two clean plastic sheets to 2-mm (0.8-in) thickness. Line the tart tin with the pastry, pressing firmly into the edge. Trim the edge neatly. Line with greaseproof paper or foil and fill with uncooked rice or baking beads and blind bake for 20-25 minutes or until the edge is slightly golden. Remove the rice and paper and bake for a further 5 minutes. Remove from the oven and set aside to cool.

For the frangipane, cream the butter and sugar together until pale and creamy. Add the eggs one at a time, beating well after each addition. Beat in the vanilla. Fold in the almond meal and flour.

Fill the cooled tart shell with the frangipane, smooth out the surface, then dot the entire surface with whole macadamia nuts. Don't push them into the batter too much or they will disappear when the batter cooks. Bake for 25-30 minutes or until the frangipane is golden.

Remove from the oven and leave to cool until just warm. Bring the apricot jam mixture to the boil. Stir until well blended and slightly thickened. You don't want a watery mixture. Brush this generously over the surface of the tart a few times to create a 2-mm (0.8-in) layer, then sprinkle on thyme leaves.

Serve with your favourite vanilla ice cream.

Sugee Bundt Cake with Cinnamon Sugar

SERVES 10-12

This cake brings back loads of childhood memories! It's essentially a butter-based cake with a good proportion of semolina. It looks brilliant baked in a bundt tin! I like eating the cake slightly warm.

100 g (3.5 oz) almond meal
50 g (⅓ cup) self-raising flour
½ teaspoon salt
¼ tsp baking soda
250 g (8.8 oz) unsalted butter
220 g (1 cup) caster sugar
7 egg yokes
2 teaspoons vanilla extract
2 teaspoons rum
125 ml (½ cup) milk
200 g (1 cup) fine semolina
3 egg whites

FOR DUSTING
1 teaspoon icing sugar
¾ teaspoon cinnamon

Preheat your oven to 160°C (320°F). Butter and flour a 21.5 x 7.5 cm (6-cup) bundt tin or, if you are using a 23-cm (9-in), round cake tin, lightly grease and line with greaseproof paper.

Sift together the almond meal, flour, salt and baking soda in a bowl.

In a separate mixing bowl, whisk together the butter and sugar until light and fluffy, add the egg yolks one at a time, making sure it's well combined after each addition. Add the vanilla and rum, then gradually pour in the milk. Add the semolina and mix until just combined. Set aside.

In another bowl, whisk the egg whites until light and fluffy.

Whisk a third of the egg whites into the butter mixture until well combined. Then fold in the remaining egg whites until just combined. Finally, fold in the dry ingredients to combine.

Bake for about 50 minutes in a bundt tin and 55 minutes in a round cake tin or until a skewer inserted in the middle of the cake comes out clean. Cool in the cake tin for 10 minutes, then turn out onto a rack to cool completely.

Mix the icing sugar and cinnamon. Dust generously over the cake before serving.

Pear, Blueberry and Honey Cream Cheese Cake

SERVES 12-16

This is not your typical cheese cake. I know it sounds quite contradictory but it's buttery and rich, and at the same time, incredibly light, comforting and delicious! Honey, pear and blueberries are just your perfect combination. I find it very hard to resist cutting into it when it comes straight out of the oven. It's perfect just a little warm!

150 g (5.3 oz) frozen or fresh
   blueberries
2 ripe pears, peeled, sliced into
   16 wedges
2 tablespoons honey
125 g (4.4 oz) cream cheese
250 g (8.8 oz) unsalted butter
220 g (1 cup) caster sugar
3 eggs
1 teaspoon vanilla extract
125 g (4.4 oz) Greek yoghurt
80 ml (⅓ cup) milk
335 g (2¼ cup) self-raising flour
Pinch of salt

Preheat your oven to 160°C (320°F). Lightly grease and line a 23-cm (9-in) cake tin with greaseproof paper. Dust lightly with flour.

Before you begin, make sure all the ingredients, including the butter and cream cheese, are at room temperature.

Cream the butter, cream cheese and sugar until light and fluffy. Add the eggs one at a time, making sure it's well combined before each addition, followed by the vanilla, yoghurt and milk. The mixture may look like it's going to curdle but don't worry, fold in the flour then the blueberries. To get a light texture, be careful not to overmix.

Fill the baking tin, smooth out the top with a spatula, then arrange the pears over the top as you wish, pushing them slightly into the batter. Drizzle over with honey.

Bake for about 1¼ hour or until a skewer inserted into the middle of the cake comes out clean. Rest for 10 minutes before turning the cake out. Serve warm on its own or with some vanilla cream.

Date, Prune, Fig, Sour Cherry & Walnut Slices

MAKES 10 MEDIUM OR 16 SMALL SLICES

I have a real weakness for a good fruit slice. This is a delicious oat-based slice that is not too sweet and has a little bit of tanginess. Feel free to change the dried fruits.

100 g (3.5 oz) dried figs, halved
100 g (3.5 oz) dried prune, halved
100 g (3.5 oz) dried dates, halved
100 g (3.5 oz) dried sour cherries
Lime or lemon zest
315 ml (1¼ cup) water
½ teaspoon baking soda
4 teaspoons lime or lemon juice
75 g (½ cup) wholemeal flour
75 g (½ cup) plain flour
100 g (½ cup) brown sugar
Pinch of salt
200 g (7 oz) cold unsalted
   butter, diced (see note)
150 g (5.3 oz) rolled oats
35 g (1/2 cup) dried shredded
   coconut
100 g (3.5 oz) walnut or pecan,
   roasted and roughly chopped
½ teaspoon ground cinnamon

Preheat your oven to 180°C (355°F). Lightly butter and line a 20-cm (8-in) square baking tin with greaseproof paper.

To make the filling, place all the dried fruit, zest, water and baking soda in a saucepan. Bring to the boil, then lower to a simmer and cook until the fruit softens, the liquid evaporates but the mixture is still moist. This will take about 20-30 minutes depending on the quality of the dried fruit.

Add the juice and stir to combine. I use the back of a spoon to mash up the tougher pieces of fruit. Don't mash them all together as you don't want to lose the individual flavours of the fruits. Set aside to cool.

In a food processor, blitz the flours, brown sugar and salt for about 10 seconds. Add the diced butter and blitz until it resembles coarse breadcrumbs. Add the rolled oats and shredded coconut and pulse a couple of times. Separate the mixture into two. Place two-thirds into the baking tin and press down firmly to form an even layer. Spread the cooled fruit mixture evenly over the top. Toss the walnut and cinnamon with the remaining third of the crumbed mixture and evenly spread over the fruit mixture. Press down to form an even layer.

Bake for about 30 minutes until golden.

Allow to cool completely before cutting into your desired size. Store in an airtight container.

Note: Remove your butter from the fridge and leave it at room temperature for about 20 minutes. If you're in a warm climate, 5 minutes will be sufficient.

Flourless Vanilla Almond Cake

SERVES 12

This is a lovely, rich gluten-free recipe. No frills, just delicious! It reminds me of the buttery coconut tarts from the Chinese bakeries in Singapore which I just love!

190 g (6.7 oz) almond meal
150 g (¾ cup) caster sugar
¼ teaspoon salt
70 g (2.5 oz) dried shredded
   coconut or 100 g (3.5 oz)
   freshly grated coconut
4 eggs
2 teaspoons vanilla extract
150 g (5.3 oz) unsalted butter,
   melted and cooled
20 g (scant ¼ cup) almond flakes
Icing sugar for dusting

Preheat your oven to 180°C (355°F). Lightly grease a 23-cm (9-in) cake tin, then dust with rice flour or line with greaseproof paper.

In a large mixing bowl, combine the almond meal, sugar, salt and coconut.

In a separate mixing bowl, whisk together the eggs and vanilla extract until well combined. Drizzle in the cooled butter and whisk until combined. Pour into the dry mix and stir until well combined. Pour into the prepared cake tin and scatter over the almond flakes.

Bake for about 40 minutes or until the cake is golden. The cake is cooked when a skewer inserted into the middle of the cake comes out clean.

Cool in the cake tin. Remove onto a plate, top side up. Dust with icing sugar and serve.

Pear and Custard Biscuits

MAKES 24-30 DEPENDING ON SIZE

This recipe came about by an act of desperation when I had leftover pastry dough and some custard in the fridge. The family had cleaned out the pantry of snacks and asked me to bake them something delicious, but it had to be quick! I had some ripe pears in the fruit bowl and figured the three elements would go rather well together. Within 30 minutes, these little morsels were out of the oven. They are a bit like a biscuit, a bit like a shortcake and a bit like a tart. Very moreish and super easy to make.

2-3 ripe pears, peeled, halved
   and thinly sliced
Raw sugar

VANILLA CUSTARD
200 ml (⅘ cup) full cream milk
1 vanilla bean, seeds scraped
40 g (1.4 oz) caster sugar
15 g (0.5 oz) cornflour
2 egg yolks

BISCUIT DOUGH
175 g (6.2 oz) plain flour
75 g (½ cup) wholemeal flour
Pinch of salt
150 g (5.3 oz) cold unsalted
   butter, cubed
1 heaped tablespoon icing sugar
1 teaspoon cinnamon

Preheat your oven to 180°C (355°F). Line a couple of baking sheets with greaseproof paper.

Start by making the vanilla custard. Place the milk and vanilla seeds in a small saucepan and bring to the boil. Immediately remove from the heat and set aside.

In a separate mixing bowl, whisk together the sugar, cornflour and egg yolks until pale and creamy. Gradually whisk in all the hot milk. Return the mixture back into the saucepan and stir over medium heat until the mixture thickens and the rawness of the cornflour disappears. Remove from the heat and pour into a glass bowl, line some cling film directly on top of the custard and refrigerate to cool.

Now for the biscuit dough. Place both flours and salt in a food processor. Blend for 10 seconds. Add the butter and pulse until it resembles coarse breadcrumbs. While the food processor is running, slowly drizzle in about 1-2 tablespoons or just enough cold water to form a dough. Wrap with cling film and rest in the refrigerator for 20 minutes.

Roll the dough out in between two plastic sheets to about 2-mm (0.8-in) thickness. Remove the top sheet, sieve the cinnamon and icing sugar all over, replace the sheet and roll over gently.

Cut out pieces using an egg-shaped cookie cutter. Place on the baking sheet. Top each pastry with a teaspoon of custard and a slice of pear. Then sprinkle over some raw sugar. Bake for 20-25 minutes until lightly coloured. Remove, cool and store in an airtight container.

Fruit and Nut Meringues

MAKES ABOUT 25 SMALL PIECES

These meringues are very moreish! You won't stop at just one and will want to keep going! The dried nuts and apricot reduce the overall sweetness of the meringues.

2 egg whites (about 60 g, 2 oz)
90 g (3.1 oz) caster sugar
¼ teaspoon rose water
25 g (0.9 oz) dried apricot, thinly sliced
25 g (0.9 oz) dried figs, thinly sliced
25 g (0.9 oz) flaked almonds, toasted
25 g (0.9 oz) pistachio kernels, toasted, roughly chopped plus extra to sprinkle over the meringues
½ teaspoon cocoa powder

Preheat your oven to 120°C (250°F). Line 2 baking sheets with greaseproof paper.

I prefer using the Swiss method of making meringues as they tend to be a little more stable. Place the egg whites and caster sugar in a heat-proof bowl sitting over a saucepan of simmering water. Stir the mixture until the sugar melts. This is when the mixture starts to run a little clearer and there are no longer granules when you rub the mixture between your fingers.

Pour the warm egg white and sugar mixture into a cake mixer with a whisk attachment. Whisk on high speed until the mixture cools and is aerated and glossy. Add the rose water and continue to whisk for a minute.

Remove the bowl from the mixer, toss in the dried fruits and nuts and fold to just combine. Sieve on the cocoa powder and, using no more than 2 strokes, fold the mixture. You only want to create some swirls of cocoa through the mixture.

Using two teaspoons, spoon small dollops onto the tray, leaving a little space in between. If you have set aside some chopped up pistachios, sprinkle them over now.

Bake for 1¼–1½ hours until the meringues are dry to touch and comes off the paper easily. Remove from the oven and allow to cool completely. This might take longer in more humid environments. Store in an air tight container.

Note: The baking time for meringues will differ, depending on the humidity of the environment. The higher the humidity, the longer it takes.

Cranberry and Pistachio Cookies

MAKES ABOUT 80

Everyone in my family is a big cookie fan. Not just the current mob but previous generations as well. My mother's biscuit tins were always full of several varieties of home-made cookies. It's always nice to have home-made cookies instead of store-bought ones.

250 g (8.8 oz) unsalted butter,
    at room temperature
150 g (5.3 oz) caster sugar
500 g (1.1 lbs) plain flour, sifted
1 teaspoon salt
2 teaspoons vanilla extract
    or 1 vanilla bean, seeds scraped
50 ml (3⅓ tablespoons)
    thickened cream
200 g (7 oz) dried cranberries,
    roughly chopped
100 g (3.5 oz) toasted pistachio
    kernels, roughly chopped

Preheat your oven to 170°C (338°F) degrees.

Cream the butter and sugar in a cake mixer with a paddle attachment until pale and creamy. Add the flour, salt and vanilla. With the mixer on low, pour in the cream gradually. As soon as a rough dough forms, add the cranberries and pistachios and pulse until roughly mixed.

Scrape out the dough onto a clean sheet of plastic, wrap, and let it rest for 30 minutes in the fridge.

Roll the dough out between two clean plastic sheets to about 5 mm (0.2 in) thick. Cut out shapes using your preferred cookie cutters or square off the edges and cut into 5 x 2.5-cm (2 x 1-in) rectangles. If the dough is too soft to handle, roll it out to the desired thickness, then refrigerate until firm before cutting.

Bake for about 18 minutes or until lightly golden.

Cool on a rack, then store in an airtight jar.

Cardamom, Pistachio and Cheddar Cookies
MAKES 70-80 TINY COOKIES

As much as I love a sweet cookie, savoury cookies are a nice alternative. I usually make them larger and thinner to go with dips or tiny to be served alongside nuts as a snack. These are really delicious morsels. Once you start, trust me, you won't be able to stop!

200 g (7 oz) plain flour
½ teaspoon freshly ground
  black pepper
10 green cardamom, crushed,
  shells discarded, seeds ground
½ teaspoon hot paprika or
  cayenne pepper
½ teaspoon baking powder
1 tablespoon caster sugar
50 g (1.8 oz) sharp cheddar
  cheese, finely grated
100 g (3.5 oz) unsalted butter,
  at room temperature
30 g (1 oz) toasted pistachios,
  roughly chopped

Preheat your oven to 180°C (355°F). Line two baking sheets with greaseproof paper.

Place the flour, spices, baking powder and sugar in a food processor and blitz for 10 seconds. Add the cheese and pulse until roughly combined. Toss in the butter and blitz until a dough is formed. You may need to add a tablespoon of cold water if the dough doesn't come together.

Roll the dough out between 2 large plastic sheets to 3-mm (0.1-in) thickness. Remove the top sheet, sprinkle over the pistachios, then return the plastic sheet and roll over very gently, compressing the nuts into the dough. Using cookie cutters of different shapes, cut out cookies and bake for 10–15 minutes or until lightly golden.

Notes: Cheddar can sometimes be quite difficult to grate finely. To obtain a finely grated finish, place the cheese in the freezer until it's firm, then grate. Or, blitz in a food processor until coarsely ground.

In warmer climates, to make it easier to cut out the dough, place the rolled out dough in the fridge or freezer until it firms up before cutting.

Lavender and Lemon Shortbread

MAKES 20 LOGS OR 12-16 SEGMENTS

A good shortbread is all about the butter, so invest in good-quality butter for this recipe. Shortbreads are very versatile and you can flavour them anyway you like. They are great on their own, with the zest of an orange or some toasted hazlenuts added to the mix.

2 teaspoons dried lavender
  flowers, plus extra
200 g (7 oz) unsalted butter
100g (½ cup) caster sugar, plus
  extra
1 teaspoon vanilla extract
1 teaspoon lemon zest
250 g (8.8 oz) plain flour
50 g (1.8 oz) rice flour
Pinch of salt

Preheat your oven to 160°C (320°F). Grease and line a 20-cm (8-in), square tin or the base of a round, loose-based, fluted tart tin with greaseproof paper.

Coarsely grind 2 teaspoons of lavender flowers with a tablespoon of sugar in a mortar and pestle.

You can make this recipe a number of ways, in a food processor, electric or hand mixer.

Cream the butter, sugar, vanilla, lavender and lemon zest until pale and smooth but not too aerated. Sift the flours and salt into a separate bowl. Fold this into the butter mixture using short pulses of a food processor or stir with a wooden spoon until a coarse crumb like mixture forms.

Empty into the baking tin and press down gently with your hands to form a smooth, flat layer. Using a sharp knife, score into 20 equal-sized logs for a square tin or 12-16 segments for a round tin. Then use a fork or skewer to poke holes evenly in each piece.

Bake for 40-45 minutes until a touch coloured.

Remove from the oven. While the shortbread is hot, use a sharp knife to cut all the way through along the scored lines. Sprinkle over the extra caster sugar and scatter with whole lavender flowers. Allow to cool completely, then store in an airtight container.

Viennese Fingers

MAKES 45

This is a cookie that I've been making since I was about 12 years old. It literally melts in your mouth! If you choose not to dip it in chocolate, cut a small piece of candied maraschino cherry and press it into one end. It'll be just as good.

230 g (8.1 oz) unsalted butter,
   at room temperature
60 g (2 oz) icing sugar
1½ teaspoons vanilla extract
250 g (8.8 oz) plain flour, sifted
Pinch of salt
1 tablespoon pistachio kernels,
   finely chopped
100 g (3.5 oz) dark chocolate,
   melted or 50 g (1.8 oz) milk
   chocolate and 50 g dark
   chocolate, melted separately

Preheat your oven to 180°C (355°F). Line 2 baking sheets with greaseproof paper.

Cream the butter and sugar until pale and fluffy. Mix in the vanilla. Add the flour and salt, pulse until just combined.

Fill a piping bag fitted with a 1-cm (0.4-in) star nozzle with the biscuit dough. Pipe out lengths of cookies spacing them about 2 cm (0.8 in) apart. Sprinkle over a little pistachio and bake for 10 minutes or until very lightly coloured. Remove and cool on a rack.

When the cookies have cooled, dip one or both ends into the melted chocolate and let it set on a rack. Store in an airtight cookie jar.

Note: In warmer climates, remove the butter from the fridge for about 10 minutes before using. This will help firm up the dough.

Olive Oil Crackers

MAKES 10 LARGE OR 15-20 MEDIUM

These crackers are great on their own or perfect with your selection of cheeses and dips.

300 g (10.5 oz) plain flour
1½ teaspoon baking powder
¾ teaspoon sea salt
¾ teaspoon hot or sweet paprika
¼ teaspoon coarsely ground
  chilli (optional)
¾ teaspoon caraway seeds
¾ teaspoon cracked black pepper
150 ml (⅗ cup) water
2 tablespoons olive oil plus extra
  for brushing

Preheat your oven to 180°C (355°F).

Mix all the ingredients to form a dough. Knead until smooth. Wrap the dough in cling film and rest for 30 minutes.

Roll the dough into a long sausage on greaseproof paper or a silicon baking sheet and divide into 16 pieces. Roll each piece into an oval shape of about 1.5-mm (0.6-in) thick. Place on a baking sheet lined with greaseproof paper.

Brush lightly with the extra olive oil and sprinkle over a little sea salt. Bake for 8-10 minutes or until lightly golden.

Store in an airtight container.

Blue Cheese and Black Pepper Biscuits

MAKES 70-80 TINY COOKIES

This is another great cookie to serve as snacks when you are having people over for drinks. I slot them in the same category as pretzels. Use the crumbly blue cheese versus the soft kind.

100 g (3.5 oz) blue cheese, crumbled
200 g (7.5 oz) plain flour
2 teaspoons freshly cracked black pepper
½ teaspoon baking powder
1 teaspoon caster sugar
1 teaspoon sea salt
100 g (3.5 oz) unsalted butter at room temperature
Parmesan cheese

Preheat your oven to 180°C (355°F). Line two baking sheets with greaseproof paper.

Place the flour, pepper, baking powder, sugar and salt in a food processor and blitz for 10 seconds. Add half the blue cheese and pulse until roughly combined.

Add the butter and blitz until a dough is formed. You may need to add 1–2 tablespoons of water for the dough to come together. In warmer climates, you may not need as much water.

Roll the dough out between 2 large plastic sheets into a 2-mm (0.8-in) thick rectangle. Crumble the remaining blue cheese over half the rectangle. Fold over to sandwich and roll to about 3-mm (0.1-in) thick. Using cookie cutters of different shapes, cut out cookies, then finely grate parmesan over them. Bake for 10–15 minutes or until lightly golden.

Note: In warm climates, roll out the dough and cool it in the fridge or freezer before cutting out the cookies.

Dark Chocolate and Fruit Oat Slices

MAKES 10 MEDIUM SLICES

You can never have too many recipes for slices. This is a perfect snack for lunch boxes or when you're on the go!

200 g (7 oz) unsalted butter, at room temperature
200 g (1 cup) brown sugar
2 eggs
1½ teaspoons vanilla extract
100 g (3.5 oz) plain flour
50 g (1.8 oz) wholemeal flour
Pinch of salt
200 g (7 oz) rolled oats
1½ cups dried fruit (raisins, cranberries, figs, apricots)
60 g (2 oz) 70% dark chocolate, broken into small chunks

Preheat your oven to 180°C (355°F). Lightly butter and line a 20-cm (8-in) square baking tin with greaseproof paper.

In a mixing bowl, cream the butter and sugar until light and fluffy. Whisk in the eggs one at a time along with the vanilla extract until well combined. Fold in both flours and the salt until almost combined, then toss in the oats, dried fruit and chocolate and mix until just combined.

Using a spatula, lightly press the dough into the baking tin ensuring the corners are well filled and the surface is smoothed out evenly. Score right through into 10 equal-sized logs.

Bake for about 25 minutes until lightly coloured and the centre of the slice is cooked through.

When still warm, slice over the score lines again and allow to cool. Store in an airtight container.

Cheese Straws

MAKES 16

These are absolute winners at any cocktail. The great news is that they are so simple and quick to make.

80 g (2.8 oz) cheddar cheese,
  finely grated
20 g (0.7 oz) parmesan cheese,
  finely grated
Shichimi togarashi to taste
2 square sheets good quality
  puff pastry
1 egg, beaten

Preheat your oven to 180°C (355°F). Line two baking sheets with greaseproof paper.

Mix both cheeses in a bowl. Season with shichimi togarashi, to your liking.

Working on one sheet at a time, using a pastry brush, brush the sheet of puff pastry lightly with egg wash. Then sprinkle a quarter of the cheese mixture over half the sheet. Fold over to sandwich, then use a rolling pin to gently compress. Sprinkle over a further quarter of the cheese mixture over the top. Using a sharp knife, cut into 8 lengths, then halve the lengths into 16 logs. Repeat with the remaining sheet of pastry.

Bake for 25-30 minutes or until golden. Cool and store in an airtight jar.

Variation: Place a red capsicum over an open flame to char it all over. Put in a glass bowl and cover with cling film. Once it's cool enough to handle, remove all the charred skin. Slice the capsicum into long and super-thin strips and dry them on paper towels. After you sprinkle over the cheese and cut the pastry into thin logs, place a strip of capsicum on top of each pastry and twist them into a spiral. Bake.

Ikan Bilis and Cheese Biscuits
Dried Anchovy and Cheese Biscuits

MAKES 70-80 TINY COOKIES

What can be more delicious than ikan bills and cheese cookies? These are more like a butter-based cracker and a perfect snack when you have friends over for drinks. Make them thin so they are crisp!

200 g (7 oz) plain flour
½ teaspoon freshly ground black pepper
½ teaspoon freshly ground white pepper
½ teaspoon hot paprika or cayenne pepper
½ teaspoon shichimi togarashi
½ teaspoon baking powder
1 teaspoon sea salt
1 teaspoon caster sugar
60 g (2 oz) sharp cheddar cheese, finely grated
30 g (1 oz) ikan bilis (dried anchovies), deep fried until crispy, drained on paper towels
100 g (3.5 oz) unsalted butter, at room temperature
Parmesan cheese

Preheat your oven to 180°C (355°F). Line two baking sheets with greaseproof paper.

Place the flour, spices, baking powder, salt and sugar in a food processor and blitz for 20 seconds. Add the cheddar and ikan bilis and pulse until roughly combined.

Add the butter and blitz until a dough is formed. You may need to add 1-2 tablespoons of water for the dough to come together. In warmer climates, you may not need as much water.

Roll the dough out between 2 large plastic sheets to 3-mm (0.1-in) thick. Alternatively, you can sandwich the cookie dough with the ikan bilis filling by rolling the dough out between 2 large plastic sheets until 4-mm (1.5-in) thick. Sprinkle the filling over half the dough. Fold the other half over and roll to about 2-3 mm (0.8-1.2 in) thick. Using cookie cutters of different shapes, cut out cookies, grate over some parmesan cheese and bake for 10-15 minutes or until lightly golden.

Note: To obtain a finely grated cheddar cheese, place it in the freezer until it's hard, then grate. Or, blitz in a food processor until finely ground.

In warmer climates, to make it easier to cut out the dough, cool the rolled out dough in the fridge or freezer until it's firm enough.

Most dried ikan bilis are slightly salted. Rinse them well before frying them. The ikan bilis filling can be easily substituted with dried prawns. Ensure they are coarsely processed and deep-fried until crispy before using.

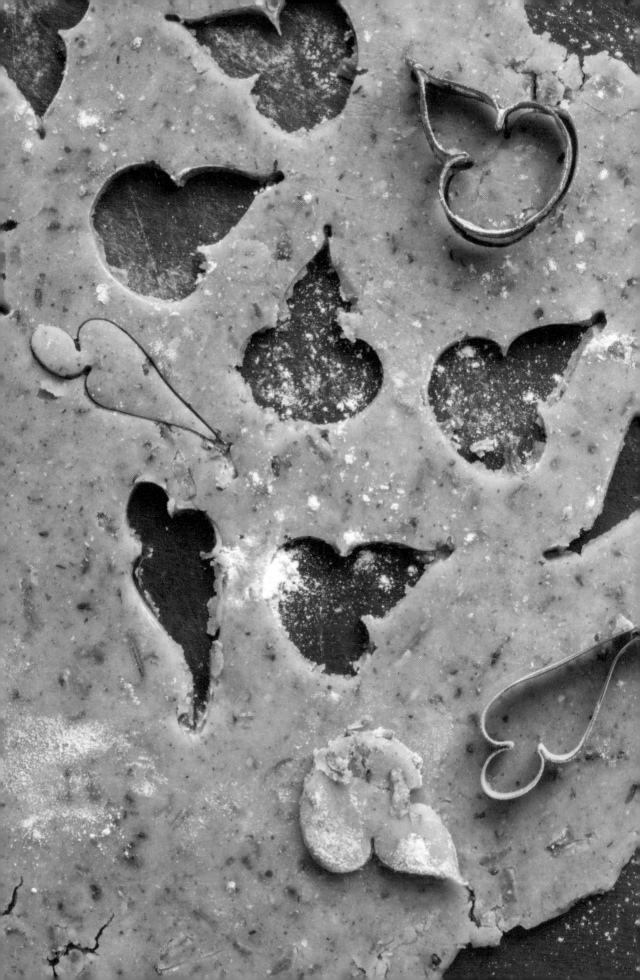

Muesli Cookies

MAKES 30

I always look out for good muesli cookies when I am in a cafe. This is a really simple recipe that can be done in a food processor. Feel free to change the nuts and dried fruit.

200 g (2 cups) rolled oats
150 g (1 cup) plain flour
¼ teaspoon baking soda
1½ teaspoons ground cinnamon
Pinch of salt
250 g (8.8 oz) unsalted butter
125 g (4.4 oz) brown sugar
1 egg
1 teaspoon vanilla extract
35 g (¼ cup) raisins
35 g (¼ cup) dried sour cherries
70 g (½ cup) dried apricots, chopped
70 g (½ cup) dried cranberries
35 g (½ cup) dried shredded coconut
70 g (½ cup) pepitas (pumpkin seeds)
50 g (½ cup) pecans or walnuts

Preheat your oven to 180°C (355°F).

Scatter the rolled oats on a baking tray and bake for 10 minutes. Remove and set aside to cool.

In a food processor, blend together the flour, baking soda, cinnamon and salt, then remove and set aside. Place the butter and sugar in the food processor and blend until pale and creamy. Add the egg and vanilla and blend until well combined. Put in the flour mixture and pulse until just combined. Include the rolled oats and the remaining ingredients and pulse until just combined.

Flour your hands and roll up golf ball sized pieces. Place on a lined baking sheet and lightly flatten each one. Bake for 20 minutes or until lightly golden. Cool and store in an airtight container.

Fruity & Nutty Toasted Muesli

MAKES ABOUT 10 CUPS (OVER 1 KG, 2.2 LB)

I love toasted muesli — not just to have for breakfast but also to snack on. I suspect that's why when I make them, they are loaded with lots of fruit and nuts which I love. As a result, you don't have to add much else to sweeten the muesli. Feel free to substitute the types of fruit and nuts I've listed in the recipe with the mixes you like.

400 g (4 cups) raw rolled oats
60 g (½ cup) white sesame
120 g (¾ cup) pepitas (pumpkin seeds)
60 g (¾ cup) almond flakes
100 g (3.5 oz) macadamia nuts, halved
100 g (3.5 oz) walnuts/pecans, roughly broken into pieces
50 g (1.8 oz) whole almonds, halved
40 g (1.4 oz) unsweetened coconut chips/flakes
2 teaspoons ground cinnamon
100 ml (²/₅ cup) apple juice
2 tablespoons oil
2 tablespoons honey
350 g (12.3 oz) mixed dried fruit (raisins, golden raisins, cranberries, apricots, figs, pears, nectarines, mulberries), chopped
2 tablespoons maple syrup

Preheat your oven to 180°C (355°F). Line an extra-large baking sheet or tin with baking paper.

In a large mixing bowl, toss together the rolled oats, sesame seeds, pepitas, almond flakes, macadamia nuts, walnuts, almonds, coconut chips and cinnamon. Add the apple juice, oil and honey and toss to combine.

Spread out onto the lined baking sheet and bake for 35 minutes, tossing through after the first 15 minutes and once more until golden. Lower the temperature to 160°C (320°F), add the dried fruits, then drizzle over the maple syrup before tossing through. Bake for a further 5 minutes.

Remove from the oven and allow to cool entirely. Store in an airtight jar.

Coconut and Chia Pudding with Gula Melaka and Passionfruit Pulp

SERVES 6-8

Chia seeds is a superfood. Though is not only easy to digest, it has a myriad of health benefits. It has low GI, is energy boosting, contributes towards healthy skin, reduces the signs of aging, maintains a healthy heart and digestive system and also builds strong bones and muscles. This is a delicious decadent pudding to have anytime of the day!

4 ripe passionfruits, halved

PUDDING
40 g (1.4 oz) chia seeds
500 ml (2 cups) coconut milk
1 teaspoon vanilla extract
1 tablespoon honey
Pinch of sea salt

SYRUP
100 g (3.5 oz) gula Melaka,
   shaved
Water

In a large glass bowl, mix together the coconut milk, vanilla, honey and salt until well combined.

Add the chia seeds and stir to combine. Cover with cling film and refrigerator for at least 6 hours.

In a small saucepan, add the shaved gula Melaka and a tablespoon or two of water. Cook over low to medium heat until the gula Melaka has melted. Pass through a sieve to remove any impurities then return to the saucepan and cook until the syrup has thickened and become syrupy. Note that the mixture will thicken a lot more when it's cool so be careful not to reduce too much.

When you are ready to serve, fill each glass with a tablespoon or two of gula Melaka syrup according to your taste. Top with a couple of spoonfuls of chia pudding. Make sure you don't stir the chia seed pudding or you will get a very sloppy mixture. Finish with a teaspoon or two of the passionfruit pulp.

This dessert can be made a day in advance and kept in a covered container in the fridge until ready to serve. Top with the passionfruit pulp just before serving.

Sago Pearls and Coconut Cream with Coconut Granita and Gula Melaka Syrup

SERVES 4-6

An oldie but still a goodie! This dessert is simple to make and is always a crowd pleaser.

200 g (7 oz) sago pearls

COCONUT GRANITA
500 ml (2 cups) coconut milk
100 g (½ cup) sugar
3 pandan leaves, torn into strips
  and knotted

GULA MELAKA SYRUP
150 g (5.3 oz) gula Melaka, shaved
2 tablespoons water

COCONUT CREAM
500 ml (2 cups) coconut milk
1 heaped tablespoon sugar
Pinch of salt
3 pandan leaves, torn into strips
  and knotted

To make the coconut granita, place all its ingredients in a saucepan over medium heat and stir until the sugar dissolves. Allow the mixture to cool, leaving the pandan leaves to infuse. When cool, remove the pandan leaves, squeezing out all the coconut milk and discard the leaves. Pour the coconut mixture into a shallow tray and place in the freezer. After an hour, remove from the freezer and use a fork to grate the surface as much as possible then returning to the freezer. Repeat this process until the entire tray is frozen but loosely grated, then transfer the granita to an airtight container and store in the freezer.

Next prepare the syrup. Place the shaved gula Melaka and water in a small saucepan and bring to the boil. Continue cooking until the gula Melaka has completely melted. Strain through a sieve then return to the saucepan and cook until the mixture has thickened slightly and becomes syrupy. Set aside.

Put the coconut milk, sugar, salt and pandan leaves in a clean, small saucepan. Cook over medium heat until the sugar and salt dissolves. Remove from the heat, leaving the pandan leaves in the saucepan to infuse. Allow to cool.

Bring another medium-sized saucepan three-quarters full of water to the boil. Slowly pour the sago into the boiling water and stir continuously to prevent the sago from clumping up. As soon as the water comes back to the boil, stop stirring. Continue cooking for about 8 minutes or until the sago is cooked to al dente with white specks in the middle. Drain through a sieve and rinse under cold water to stop the cooking and to remove all the excess starch. If you are preparing this in advance and the sago clumps together, place them in a pot of warm water and separate them by running your fingers through them. Drain well before serving.

Divide the sago into individual bowls, top with a good amount of coconut cream, drizzle with the gula Melaka syrup and spoon over some coconut granita.

Choux Puffs with Cream Cheese Yoghurt Masala

MAKES 25-30

These little cheesy morsels are my Indian-heritage take on the French gougeres, which I absolutely love!
I make them small with a little bit of filling piped into the middle so you can literally pop one in your
mouth in a go. Perfect for canapés!

FILLING

1 tablespoon cold-pressed, extra-virgin coconut oil
1 medium onion, peeled, finely diced
1 heaped teaspoon finely grated ginger
1 heaped teaspoon finely grated garlic
1 tablespoon finely chopped coriander stem and root
1 large hot green chilli, finely diced
1 teaspoon curry powder
½ teaspoon ground cumin
½ teaspoon ground coriander
½ teaspoon cinnamon
½ teaspoon hot paprika
½ teaspoon turmeric
½ teaspoon sugar
Sea salt to taste
Zest of half a lime
Squeeze of lime juice
¼ cup fresh coriander leaves, finely chopped
250 g (8.8 oz) cream cheese
100 g (3.5 oz) labneh or thick, Greek yoghurt

CHOUX PUFFS

160 ml water
1 teaspoon sea salt
1 teaspoon sugar
75 g (2.6 oz) unsalted butter
100 g plain flour
1 teaspoon cumin seeds, toasted, lightly crushed
1 large red chilli, halved, seeds removed, sliced thinly on the diagonal
2 stalks curry leaves, stems

Start by making the filling. In a medium fry pan, heat the coconut oil over medium-high heat. Fry the onion for 2-3 minutes until softened. Add the ginger, garlic, coriander stems and root, and green chilli. Cook for a further 2-3 minutes until everything wilts and softens. Put in the curry powder, cumin, coriander, cinnamon, hot paprika and turmeric, cooking on low-medium heat until well combined and fragrant. Season with sugar and salt. Transfer into a bowl then add lime zest and lime juice to taste. Finally, stir through the fresh chopped coriander.

In a separate mixing bowl, whip the cream cheese until light before folding in the yoghurt to make a pipe-able consistency. Fold in the masala leaving streaks of masala in the cream cheese. Taste and season as you wish. Place in a piping bag fitted with a ½-cm (0.2-in) nozzle and refrigerate until ready to use.

Preheat your oven to 200°C (395°F). Prepare a piping bag with a 1-cm (0.4-in), round nozzle. Line two baking trays with greaseproof paper.

To make the choux puffs, place the water, salt, sugar and butter in a medium saucepan and bring to the boil. Remove from the heat and add all the flour, stirring vigorously until all the liquid has been absorbed and there are no traces of dry flour. Place it back on the stove over medium-low heat and stir to dry out the dough. Cook until the dough comes away from the sides. This should take 3-5 minutes.

Transfer the dough to a standing cake mixer with a paddle attachment. Leave for 1 minute to cool. Beat for 30 seconds, then add the cumin, chillies and curry leaves. Once the mixture has cooled a little whilst beating, slowly drizzle in the whisked eggs a little at a time ensuring the mixture is well combined between additions. Add both cheeses and beat until you get an elastic, glossy and shiny mixture.

discarded, leaves finely
shredded
4 eggs, lightly whisked plus
1 more for glazing
1 cup gruyere cheese, grated
2 tablespoons grated pecorino

Fill the 1-cm (0.4-in) round-nozzled piping bag and pipe out small mounds of the size you wish onto the lined tray.

Dip your finger into a bowl of water and smooth out the tips of the mounds. Whisk the remaining egg with 1 tablespoon of water. Brush each mound with this glaze. Bake for about 20-25 minutes until golden. Remove from the oven and set aside to cool.

Pipe the cream cheese yoghurt filling into each puff and serve immediately.

Banana Fritters with Gula Melaka

MAKES 12-16

This was one of my favoured snacks when I was a kid. Mom used to make really fabulous ones with super-crunchy batter. How many fritters you get from this recipe depends on the size of the bananas.

6-8 small bananas, left whole or
halved lengthways
50 g (1.8 oz) gula Melaka

BATTER
150 g (1 cup) plain flour, sifted
¾ tablespoon baking powder
Good pinch of salt
250 ml (1 cup) ice-cold soda
water

Preheat a medium pot or wok filled with oil to 180°C (355°F). Line a tray with paper towels.

Mix the flour, baking powder and salt in a mixing bowl. Slowly mix in the soda water. I like using a pair of chopsticks to whisk as it prevents you from over mixing. Whatever you do, don't over mix. You should still see pockets of flour in the batter. This is okay.

Gently dip each piece of banana into the batter, allow it to drip off, then lower it straight into the hot oil. Fry until golden. Drain on paper towels. Repeat with the remaining bananas.

Place the gula Melaka and 2 tablespoons of water in a small saucepan. Cook over medium heat until the gula Melaka dissolves and mixture slightly thickens. Strain through a sieve to remove any impurities. Drizzle over the banana fritters and serve up.

Apricot and Vanilla Jam

MAKES ABOUT FOUR 180-G (6.3-OZ) JARS

Apricot season runs over the summer months. Fruit is in abundance and prices drop substantially so it's the perfect time to make jam! I actually prefer the taste of cooked apricots more than the fresh ones. Whether they are roasted or cooked down into a compote, the flavour really intensifies. This jam is also perfect over ice cream or in tarts!

1.25 kg (2.75 lbs) ripe
   apricots, washed, halved and
   seeds removed
200 g (7 oz) raw sugar
1 vanilla bean, halved, seeds
   scraped

Place the apricots, sugar, vanilla seeds and pod into a large, heavy-based saucepan. Bring to the boil. Lower the heat to medium and cook with the lid slightly covered for about 20-25 minutes until jam is of desired consistency. Make sure you stir frequently to avoid the base from catching.

While the apricot jam is cooking, sterilise four 180-g (6.3-oz) jars by washing with soapy water and rinsing well with hot water. Dry in the oven set at 120°C (250°F) for 15-20 minutes.

While the jam is still hot (about 85°C, 185°F), fill the jars carefully. Tighten with the lids and invert for 1 minute. When the jam cools, it will create a vacuum seal.

Label your jams with the date of bottling. It's best to consume your jam as soon as possible but if prepared the right way, these jams can keep for 12+ months if stored in a cool and dry place.

Strawberry and Lime Jam

MAKES ABOUT FOUR 180-G (6.3-OZ) JARS

When strawberry season arrives in Australia, they can be as cheap as A$1 for a 250 g (8.8-oz) punnet. Apart from eating copious amounts of them fresh, I love turning them into compotes, jams or relishes. This is a lovely, simple recipe that has the addition of lime.

A friend of mine, who has a great love of making jams, shared with me that if you bake the strawberries in the oven beforehand, the flavours will intensify. So I have used his method in this recipe.

I prefer my relishes and jams less sweet so feel free to adjust the amount of sugar you add to the recipe. You might also need to adjust this if your strawberries aren't particularly sweet. However, please ensure additional sugar doesn't mask the natural flavour of the strawberries and lime.

1 kg (2.2 lbs) strawberries,
  hulled, rinsed and left to dry
100 g (3.5 oz) raw sugar
8 strips of lime rind
4 teaspoons lime juice

Preheat your oven to 200°C (395°F).

Place the strawberries on a baking tray lined with greaseproof paper. Scatter over about 60 g (2 oz) of the sugar. Bake in the hot oven for 25 minutes.

Remove the strawberries from the oven and empty all contents, including the juices, into a medium, heavy-based saucepan. Throw in the lime rind, and pour in the remaining sugar and lime juice. Place the saucepan over low to medium heat and let it simmer for 30 minutes, stirring every 5 minutes until you've reached your desired consistency.

While the strawberry jam is cooking, sterilise four 180-g (6.3-oz) jars by washing with soapy water and rinsing well with hot water. Dry in a 120°C (250°F) oven for 15-20 minutes.

While the jam is still hot (about 85°C, 18°F), fill the jars carefully. Tighten with the lids and invert for 1 minute. When the jam cools, it will create a vacuum seal.

Label your jams with the date of bottling. It's best to consume your jam as soon as possible but if prepared the right way, these jams can keep for 12+ months if stored in a cool and dry place.

INDEX

EXTRA GOODIES

Audra on TV and the web *I am excited to be one of the three judges on MasterChef Singapore. Having been through the experience of MasterChef Australia and now building my own brand in the food business, it's a great opportunity to inspire and mentor.*

"Tasty Conversations" is my own short-form cooking series produced by the great folks at Carnival Productions in Sydney. I am delighted that this series is broadcasted on SBS in Australia and on fyi broadcasting across Asia. Look out for online versions of this series on http://tastyconversations.com.au. Series 2 features absolutely everything I love about Singaporean food. Some of the recipes included from my books are my mouthwatering Laksa, Nonya Chicken Curry and Raw Salmon with Szechuan Dressing.

Audra's Food Products *I have launched a range of food products utilising the best of Australian seasonal produce with an intent to fully support local growers. Each jar of relish and jam encapsulates my passion for food and pure love of cooking. The range currently includes a Plum Chilli Relish, perfect for dolloping over a juicy beef burger or as a perfect accompaniment to cheeses; a Pickled Green Chilli Mayo which, when smothered in a pulled pork slider, takes you to a very happy place; and finally, my Vanilla Bean Fig Jam which is perfect on top of rye toast, as a topping for a tart, with cheese or just dolloped over your favourite vanilla ice-cream. All my products are natural, free from preservatives and colouring, and gluten free. They are currently available at Hubers Butchery at Dempsey in Singapore. For stockists in Australia, please contact info@audramorrice.com.au*

Audra Caters *Food is a way to invigorate the senses, excite the palate and warm the spirit, giving great satisfaction and comfort to your dining experience. This is what my catering is all about.*

I currently cater for both corporate and private-dining events in Sydney, Australia. Inspired largely by my rich cultural heritage from growing up in Singapore and my love for food, I also gather inspiration from my travels and the people I meet.

My specialty dining event, Cook & Feast, is an intimate cooking class coupled with a dining experience where diners not only learn to cook some of my dishes but also learn about their origins and heritage.

Regular pop-up dinners are an ongoing activity featuring my eclectic Asian style of cooking!

For all catering enquiries, please contact info@audramorrice.com.au.